Humane Homeschooling

Astronomical Tutor

Published by Astronomical Tutor, 2024.

While every precaution has been taken in the preparation of this book, the publisher assumes no responsibility for errors or omissions, or for damages resulting from the use of the information contained herein.

HUMANE HOMESCHOOLING

First edition. November 1, 2024.

Copyright © 2024 Astronomical Tutor.

ISBN: 979-8227424327

Written by Astronomical Tutor.

I dedicate this book to all the current school choice and homeschool advocates that are doing their very best to fight the stigma that a certain population of students is destined to be excluded from the essential human right of access to an education.

Letter to the Reader

Dear Reader,

In the midst of an ongoing education crisis, where schools are increasingly adopting curricula that fall short in teaching fundamental reading and math skills, many parents are faced with a daunting choice. As you navigate this challenging landscape, you may find yourself considering homeschooling as a viable alternative to ensure your child's education meets their needs. This guide is designed to empower and support you on this journey.

Homeschooling, often viewed as a last resort, can indeed be a profound opportunity for both you and your child. At its core, education is not merely a series of academic lessons; it is an extension of caregiving. It is an opportunity to foster growth, nurture curiosity, and build a strong foundation for lifelong learning. As a parent, you are uniquely positioned to provide this care and support, given your deep understanding of your child's needs, strengths, and interests.

This guide aims to provide you with practical tools and insights to navigate the homeschooling landscape effectively. We will explore how to develop and implement a curriculum that addresses your child's unique learning needs while aligning with humane and ethical educational practices. You will learn how to create a nurturing and engaging learning environment, understand the importance of integrating diverse perspectives, and harness the power of your teaching strengths to support your child's educational journey.

By embracing the role of educator, you are not merely stepping into a new role; you are extending the very essence of caregiving that defines your relationship with your child. Homeschooling is not just about delivering academic content—it is about fostering a supportive, engaging, and empathetic learning experience. Your commitment to this process can transform the challenges of today's education system into an opportunity for meaningful and personalized learning.

As you embark on this journey, remember that you are not alone. Many parents are navigating similar challenges, and the resources and strategies outlined in this guide are designed to support you every step of the way. Your dedication to your child's education is a testament to your love and commitment, and it positions you to be the best advocate and educator for your child.

Thank you for choosing to invest in your child's education. Together, we can turn the challenges of today's educational landscape into a pathway for success, growth, and discovery. Your role as a homeschool educator is not just a necessity but a powerful choice that reflects your dedication to your child's future.

Definition of a Humane Homeschool

A humane homeschool is an educational approach that prioritizes the wellbeing and individual needs of each student while integrating a rich tapestry of principles grounded in biodiversity, neurodiversity, ethics, and environmental education. It fosters a nurturing and inclusive learning environment that respects and celebrates the uniqueness of each learner and promotes a deep connection to the natural world and ethical values.

Core Principles

Biodiversity

Embracing Diversity: A humane homeschool recognizes and values the diversity of life and perspectives, reflecting this appreciation in the curriculum and learning environment. It integrates lessons that highlight the interconnectedness of all living things and encourages students to explore and respect different cultures, species, and ecosystems.

Educational Content: Incorporate educational materials and activities that emphasize the importance of biodiversity and conservation, helping students understand the role of different species in maintaining ecological balance.

Neurodiversity

Inclusive Learning: A humane homeschool is grounded in the principles of neurodiversity, acknowledging that each student's cognitive and emotional processing is unique. It adapts teaching methods and materials to accommodate a wide range of learning styles and needs, ensuring that every student has the opportunity to thrive.

StrengthBased Approach: Emphasize the strengths and abilities of neurodivergent students, tailoring instruction to leverage their individual talents and support their specific learning needs.

Ethics

Respect and Empathy: Ethical principles underpin the humane homeschool approach, fostering an environment where respect, empathy, and integrity are paramount. Students are encouraged to engage in ethical reasoning, understand their responsibilities towards others, and develop a strong sense of moral values.

Critical Thinking: Teach students to think critically about ethical issues, including social justice, fairness, and personal responsibility. This helps them navigate complex moral questions and become thoughtful, engaged citizens.

Environmental Education

Connection to Nature: A humane homeschool integrates environmental education to deepen students' understanding of their relationship with the natural world. This includes lessons on sustainability, conservation, and the impact of human activities on the environment.

HandsOn Learning: Provide opportunities for hands on learning through outdoor activities, nature exploration, and environmental projects that foster a sense of stewardship and connection to the earth.

Practical Implementation

Curriculum Design

Integrative Approach: Design a curriculum that weaves together themes of biodiversity, neurodiversity, ethics, and environmental education. Create interdisciplinary lessons that connect these principles with core academic subjects.

Diverse Resources: Use a variety of educational resources, including books, multimedia materials, and community partnerships, to support a holistic understanding of these concepts.

Learning Environment

Inclusive Space: Create a learning environment that is welcoming and accommodating to all students, with flexible seating arrangements, sensory friendly materials, and access to diverse learning tools.

EcoFriendly Practices: Implement eco friendly practices within the homeschool setting, such as recycling, energy conservation, and sustainable materials.

Community Engagement

Local Partnerships: Engage with local organizations, nature centers, and community groups to provide real world experiences and broaden students' perspectives.

Service Learning: Incorporate service learning projects that allow students to apply their knowledge and skills in ways that benefit the community and the environment.

Ongoing Reflection

Feedback and Growth: Continuously seek feedback from students and adapt the learning environment and curriculum to better meet their needs and reflect the principles of a humane homeschool.

Professional Development: Stay informed about best practices in education and engage in ongoing professional development to enhance your ability to provide a high-quality, humane educational experience.

This definition provides a comprehensive framework for creating a humane homeschool that is inclusive, ethical, and connected to the broader world. It emphasizes the importance of recognizing and supporting each student's unique needs while fostering a deep respect for the environment and diverse perspectives.

The Opposite of a Humane Homeschool

The opposite of a humane homeschool can be characterized by several key features that contrast sharply with the principles of a humane and inclusive educational environment.

Exclusionary Practices

Lack of Inclusivity: An inhumane homeschool may fail to embrace diversity in learning needs, backgrounds, and abilities. It might not accommodate students with disabilities or neurodivergent traits, potentially creating an environment where some students feel unsupported or marginalized.

Rigid Curriculum: It may use a one-size-fits-all approach to education, lacking flexibility to adapt to individual learning styles or needs. This rigidity can overlook the unique strengths and challenges of each student.

Authoritarian Methods

Lack of Autonomy: An authoritarian approach may not value or foster student autonomy and self direction. Instead of encouraging independent thinking and self expression, it may impose strict control and limit opportunities for students to make choices about their learning.

Limited Student Input: There might be minimal consideration for student interests, preferences, or feedback, resulting in a less engaging and less responsive learning environment.

Neglect of Emotional and Social Needs

Ignoring Wellbeing: A non-human homeschool might not address the emotional, social, or psychological needs of students. It may prioritize academic achievement over personal growth and wellbeing, leading to a lack of support for mental health and social development.

Minimal Support Systems: It may lack resources or systems for providing social and emotional support, such as counseling or peer interactions, which are crucial for a well rounded educational experience.

Disregard for Ethical Practices

Unethical Content and Methods: An opposite approach may include educational practices that are ethically questionable, such as using outdated or biased materials, or failing to teach critical thinking and ethical reasoning.

NonTransparent Policies: There might be a lack of transparency in educational policies and practices, leading to potential exploitation or unfair treatment of students.

Lack of Flexibility and Adaptability

Inflexible Structure: An inflexible educational structure that does not adapt to changes in a student's needs or circumstances can hinder effective learning and personal growth. It may also lack responsiveness to evolving educational standards or advancements in teaching methods.

Resistance to Change: A non-human homeschool might resist incorporating new research or best practices in education, limiting its effectiveness and relevance.

Insufficient Community Engagement

Isolation: A non-human homeschool may operate in isolation, without engaging with the broader educational community or seeking external support and resources. This can lead to a lack of collaboration, shared learning, and mutual support among homeschooling families.

Minimal Resource Sharing: There may be limited efforts to build or participate in resource centers, coops, or community networks that could enhance the homeschooling experience.

The opposite of a humane homeschool is characterized by exclusionary practices, authoritarian methods, neglect of emotional and social needs, disregard for ethical practices, lack of flexibility, and insufficient community engagement. In contrast, a humane homeschool values inclusivity, fosters autonomy, supports emotional wellbeing, adheres to ethical standards, remains adaptable, and actively engages with the community. By understanding these differences, parents can better appreciate and strive to create a supportive, respectful, and effective learning environment for their children.

A Humane Homeschool Is Inclusive, Not Exclusionary

A humane homeschool is designed to be inclusive and accommodating, reflecting a deep understanding and appreciation of biodiversity, neurodiversity, and the diverse needs of all learners.

Embracing Biodiversity

Understanding Diversity in Learning: Just as biodiversity recognizes the variety of life forms in an ecosystem, a humane homeschool acknowledges the diverse learning styles, interests, and strengths of each student. This approach ensures that every student has the opportunity to thrive in an environment that supports their unique needs.

Creating an Inclusive Curriculum: A humane homeschool incorporates materials and activities that reflect a range of cultures, perspectives, and experiences. This includes diverse literature, global history, and scientific concepts that celebrate the richness of our world.

Valuing Neurodiversity

Recognizing Unique Learning Profiles: Neurodiversity appreciates the variety in cognitive processing and learning styles. A humane homeschool recognizes that students may have different ways of understanding and interacting with information, including those with dyslexia, ADHD, autism, and other neurodivergent traits.

Tailoring Educational Approaches: By incorporating strategies and tools that cater to different neurotypes, such as multisensory learning, structured literacy, and flexible scheduling, a humane homeschool ensures that each student's cognitive and emotional needs are met.

Accommodating Disabilities

Providing Accessibility and Support: A humane homeschool actively works to accommodate disabilities, ensuring that all students have access to the resources and support they need to succeed. This includes modifying materials, providing assistive technologies, and adapting teaching methods to suit each student's abilities.

Fostering an Inclusive Environment: Creating a supportive and understanding environment is key. This involves encouraging empathy, promoting positive interactions, and ensuring that all students feel valued and included in the learning process.

Promoting Inclusivity Through Practice

Customized Learning Plans: Develop individualized learning plans that cater to each student's needs, strengths, and challenges. This approach helps address specific learning requirements and supports academic and personal growth.

Open Communication: Maintain open lines of communication with students and their families to understand their needs and preferences. This helps in adapting teaching methods and resources to be more effective and inclusive.

Ongoing Professional Development: Engage in ongoing learning about inclusive education practices, disability rights, and neurodiversity. This knowledge equips parents and educators to better support all students.

Building a Supportive Community

Collaborative Efforts: Work with local organizations, support groups, and educational resources that focus on inclusivity and support for diverse learners. This collaboration can provide additional resources and foster a broader community of understanding.

Sharing Knowledge and Resources: Create and participate in communities or networks where experiences, strategies, and resources are shared. This helps in continuously improving and adapting inclusive practices.

A humane homeschool is characterized by its commitment to inclusivity, ensuring that all students, regardless of their background, abilities, or learning styles, are supported and valued. By embracing biodiversity, neurodiversity, and accommodating disabilities, parents can create an educational environment that is enriching, equitable, and empowering for every child. This approach not only supports academic success but also nurtures a sense of belonging and respect for the diverse capabilities of all learners.

Researching Parenting and School Philosophy

Define Your Philosophy

Personal Values: Reflect on your personal values and beliefs about education, child development, and family life.

Educational Goals: Identify what you want your child to achieve academically, socially, and emotionally.

Philosophical Frameworks: Research various educational philosophies (e.g., Montessori, Waldorf, traditional, progressive) and parenting styles (e.g., authoritative, permissive, authoritative) to see what aligns with your values.

Explore Educational Theories

Academic Resources: Read books, articles, and research papers on educational theories and parenting approaches.

Educational Websites: Visit reputable educational websites and forums that discuss different educational philosophies and their practical applications.

Consult with Experts

Parenting Coaches: Seek advice from parenting coaches or educational consultants who can provide guidance based on your philosophical preferences.

Local Parent Groups: Join local or online parent groups to discuss educational philosophies and hear from other parents about their experiences.

Researching Local School Districts

Gather Information

School Websites: Visit the websites of local school districts to review their mission statements, educational programs, and philosophy.

School Reviews: Look for reviews and ratings of local schools from parents and educational review sites.

District Policies: Check the district's policies on curriculum, student support services, and extracurricular activities.

Evaluate Alignment

Curriculum and Instruction: Compare the curriculum and instructional methods of the local schools with your educational philosophy. For instance, if you value a handson, experiential approach, look for schools with project based learning.

Support Services: Assess the availability of support services, such as special education, counseling, and enrichment programs, to ensure they align with your expectations.

Visit Schools

School Tours: Arrange visits to local schools to observe classrooms, meet teachers, and get a feel for the school environment.

Parent Meetings: Attend school board meetings or parent teacher association (PTA) meetings to ask questions and learn more about the school's practices.

Exploring School Choice Options

Types of School Choices

Charter Schools: Explore charter schools, which often have specialized programs or unique educational approaches.

Private Schools: Research private schools that may offer alternative educational philosophies or smaller class sizes.

Magnet Schools: Look into magnet schools that focus on specific areas such as STEM, arts, or language immersion.

Homeschooling: Consider homeschooling if local schools do not meet your educational philosophy or if you want a more personalized approach.

Researching Options

School Directories: Use online directories and resources to find information about various school choice options in your area.

Parent Reviews: Read reviews from other parents who have experience with the schools or programs you are considering.

Evaluate and Decide

Pros and Cons: Weigh the pros and cons of each option based on your family's needs and values.

Enrollment Processes: Understand the enrollment procedures, deadlines, and any requirements for each school choice option.

Starting a Humane Homeschool

Legal and Administrative Requirements

State Regulations: Research your state's homeschooling laws and regulations, including notification requirements, curriculum standards, and assessment methods.

Documentation: Prepare necessary documentation, such as an intent to homeschool letter and a recordkeeping system for educational progress.

Curriculum Planning

Educational Philosophy: Develop a curriculum that aligns with your educational philosophy and addresses your child's learning needs and interests.

Resources: Gather educational resources, including textbooks, workbooks, online materials, and manipulatives. Consider using structured literacy and math programs if those align with your educational goals.

Subject Areas: Plan for a comprehensive curriculum covering core subjects (language arts, math, science, social studies) and additional areas such as art, physical education, and social emotional learning.

Daily Schedule and Learning Environment

Routine: Create a daily schedule that balances structured learning with flexible, handson activities.

Learning Space: Design a dedicated learning space that is conducive to focused and engaging study.

Assessing Progress

Regular Assessments: Implement regular assessments to track your child's academic progress and adjust the curriculum as needed.

Feedback: Seek feedback from your child and adjust the learning approach to ensure it meets their needs and interests.

Community and Support

Support Networks: Join homeschooling communities or coops to connect with other homeschooling families and access shared resources and social opportunities.

Professional Support: Consider consulting with educational specialists or tutors if additional support is needed for specific subjects or learning needs.

By researching and aligning your parenting and educational philosophy with local school districts, exploring school choice options, and considering a humane homeschooling approach, you can ensure that your child's educational experience is tailored to your values and meets their unique needs. This process involves careful evaluation, planning, and ongoing adjustment to create an enriching and supportive learning environment for your child.

Roles of Parents in Homeschooling

In a homeschooling setting, parents take on multiple roles typically distributed among various school staff in traditional educational environments. This comprehensive involvement allows parents to tailor their child's education according to individual needs, preferences, and goals.

Board of Education

Curriculum Oversight: As the board of education, parents are responsible for selecting and overseeing the curriculum. They ensure that educational standards are met and that the content is appropriate for their child's age and developmental stage.

Policy Decisions: Parents make decisions about educational policies, such as grading practices, evaluation methods, and instructional approaches.

Principal

Daily Operations: In the role of principal, parents manage the daytoday operations of the homeschooling environment, including scheduling, setting academic goals, and organizing learning activities.

Resource Management: Parents allocate resources, including educational materials and tools, and oversee the implementation of the curriculum.

Counselor

Emotional Support: As counselors, parents provide emotional and social support, addressing any concerns or challenges that arise during the learning process.

Career and Academic Guidance: Parents help guide their child's academic and career interests, offering advice on future goals and potential pathways.

Administrator

Record Keeping: Parents handle administrative tasks such as maintaining records of progress, attendance, and assessments. They ensure that all required documentation is completed and uptodate.

Communication: Parents manage communication with any outside resources or agencies, including local education authorities or extracurricular activity providers.

Educator

Instruction: As educators, parents deliver instruction in various subjects, adapting their teaching methods to their child's learning style and needs.

Assessment: Parents assess their child's understanding and progress through tests, projects, and informal evaluations, adjusting the curriculum as necessary.

Deciding on Subject Delivery

Teaching vs. Outsourcing

Assessing Expertise: Parents evaluate their own expertise and comfort level with different subjects. If they feel confident in teaching a subject, they may choose to do so themselves.

Outsourcing: For subjects where the parent feels less confident or requires additional support, they can consider outsourcing. This could involve hiring tutors, enrolling the child in online courses, or attending local classes or workshops.

Areas of Responsibility

Gifted Education

Enrichment Activities: Parents design and provide enrichment activities that challenge and stimulate gifted learners, adapting instruction to match their advanced skills and interests.

Accommodations

Individualized Support: Parents implement accommodations to support any learning difficulties or disabilities, ensuring that their child has the necessary resources and modifications for success.

Social and Emotional Learning (SEL)

Developing Skills: Parents integrate SEL into daily activities, focusing on emotional intelligence, interpersonal skills, and resilience. They create a supportive environment that fosters positive social interactions and self awareness.

Sex Education

AgeAppropriate Lessons: Parents provide sex education that is age appropriate and aligns with their family values. This includes discussing topics related to human development, relationships, and personal safety.

Physical Education

Activity Planning: Parents plan and implement physical education activities that promote physical health, fitness, and coordination. This can include organized sports, exercise routines, and outdoor activities.

Art and Music Education

Creative Expression: Parents include art and music education through hands-on projects, lessons in various art forms, and exposure to different musical styles and instruments.

Sports Education

Skill Development: Parents may introduce sports education by organizing sports activities, encouraging participation in community sports teams, or providing resources for skill development.

Business and Financial Literacy

Practical Skills: Parents teach business and financial literacy by incorporating lessons on budgeting, saving, investing, and entrepreneurial skills. Real Life experiences, such as managing allowances or starting small projects, can be used to reinforce these concepts.

Media Literacy

Critical Analysis: Parents educate their child on media literacy, teaching them to critically analyze media sources, understand digital citizenship, and navigate online information responsibly.

In homeschooling, parents assume the multifaceted roles of the board of education, principal, counselor, administrator, and educator. This comprehensive involvement allows them to make informed decisions about their child's education, including whether to teach a subject themselves or seek external support. Parents are responsible for a wide range of educational areas, including gifted education, accommodations, social and emotional learning, and various subjects such as physical education, art, music, sports, business, and media literacy. By balancing these responsibilities, parents can create a customized and supportive learning environment that addresses their child's unique needs and interests.

Getting Started:

Starting an independent humane homeschool involves several important considerations across logistics, economics, and long term implications.

Logistics

Legal Requirements

State Regulations: Research your state's homeschooling laws and regulations, which may include registering as a homeschooler, submitting an intent to homeschool, or adhering to specific curriculum standards.

Record Keeping: Maintain detailed records of educational activities, attendance, and assessments to comply with state requirements and track your child's progress.

Curriculum Development

Curriculum Planning: Develop or select a curriculum that aligns with your educational philosophy and meets your child's learning needs. This includes planning for core subjects (language arts, math, science, social studies) and supplementary subjects (art, physical education).

Resource Acquisition: Gather necessary educational materials such as textbooks, workbooks, educational software, and manipulatives. Consider both purchased resources and free or low cost online materials.

Learning Environment

Space: Designate a dedicated learning space that is comfortable, organized, and conducive to focused study. This can be a separate room or a designated area within your home.

Schedule: Create a daily and weekly schedule that balances structured learning with flexibility for exploration and handson activities. Include time for breaks, physical activity, and social interactions.

Assessment and Evaluation

Progress Monitoring: Implement regular assessments to evaluate your child's academic progress and adjust the curriculum as needed. This may include tests, projects, and informal evaluations.

Feedback: Regularly solicit feedback from your child about their learning experience and make adjustments to ensure it remains engaging and effective.

Economics

Initial Costs

Curriculum and Materials: Budget for the cost of curriculum materials, educational resources, and any initial setup expenses for the learning environment.

Technology: Consider costs for technology such as computers, printers, and educational software. If using online resources, factor in internet costs and subscription fees.

Ongoing Expenses

Supplies: Budget for ongoing expenses such as art supplies, books, and other educational materials.

Extracurricular Activities: Include costs for extracurricular activities, field trips, and social events that provide enrichment and socialization opportunities.

Opportunity Costs

Parental Time: Consider the time investment required for planning, teaching, and managing the homeschool. This may impact the ability to pursue other professional or personal activities.

Potential Income Loss: If one parent plans to stay home fulltime to manage homeschooling, there may be an impact on family income.

Financial Planning

Savings and Budgeting: Develop a detailed budget that accounts for both initial and ongoing expenses. Explore potential financial assistance or grants available for homeschooling families.

LongTerm Financial Considerations: Consider how homeschooling may affect long term financial goals, such as retirement savings or educational savings accounts.

LongTerm Pros and Cons

Pros

Customized Education: Tailor the curriculum to meet your child's individual learning style, interests, and pace, which can enhance engagement and academic success.

Flexibility: Enjoy flexibility in scheduling, allowing for personalized learning experiences and the ability to travel or pursue unique opportunities.

Strong ParentChild Bond: Strengthen the bond with your child through close involvement in their education and daily activities.

Safe Learning Environment: Create a controlled learning environment that can be more conducive to your child's needs, especially if they have special learning requirements.

Cons

Time Commitment: Managing a homeschool requires a significant time investment for planning, teaching, and administrative tasks.

Financial Strain: Covering the costs of materials, resources, and potential lost income can be financially challenging.

Socialization: While homeschool can offer personalized socialization opportunities, it requires effort to ensure that your child interacts with peers and engages in social activities.

Parental Stress: Balancing the roles of teacher, parent, and possibly maintaining a job can lead to stress and burnout.

Key Considerations for DecisionMaking

Family Needs and Dynamics

Assess Family Roles: Evaluate how homeschooling fits into your family's daily life and dynamics. Consider how it will impact other family members and their routines.

Evaluate Support Systems: Determine if you have a support network in place, including access to homeschooling communities, coops, or local resources.

Educational Goals

Set Clear Objectives: Define your educational goals for your child and how homeschooling aligns with these objectives. Consider long term outcomes, including high school graduation and college or career readiness.

Adaptability and Flexibility

Be Prepared to Adapt: Understand that homeschooling requires flexibility and adaptability. Be willing to adjust your approach based on your child's needs and feedback.

By carefully considering these aspects, parents can make informed decisions about starting an independent humane homeschool, ensuring that it aligns with their values, meets their child's needs, and fits within their family's logistical and financial capacity.

Teaching as Caregiving

Nurturing Growth

Emotional Support: Like caregiving, teaching involves providing emotional support and creating a safe environment where a child feels valued and understood. This supportive atmosphere is crucial for effective learning.

Individual Attention: Both roles require attentive, individualized interactions that cater to a child's unique needs, interests, and developmental stage.

Guidance and Modeling

Role Modeling: Just as caregivers model behaviors and values, teachers demonstrate skills, problem solving approaches, and attitudes towards learning. This modeling helps children understand expectations and learn by observation.

Encouragement: Caregivers and teachers both use encouragement to build confidence and motivate children, fostering a growth mindset and resilience.

Gradual Release of Responsibility

Concept Overview

Definition: The gradual release of responsibility is an instructional approach where the teacher initially provides substantial support and guidance, gradually transferring the responsibility for learning to the student as their competence grows.

Stages:

I Do: The teacher demonstrates the task or concept, providing clear explanations and modeling the desired behavior or skill.

We Do: The teacher and students work together on the task, with the teacher providing support and feedback while the students actively participate.

You Do Together: Students work in small groups or pairs, with the teacher offering minimal guidance as students apply the skills collaboratively.

You Do: Students independently complete the task or demonstrate their understanding, with the teacher providing feedback as needed.

Application in Homeschooling

Tailored Support: In a humane homeschool, this approach allows parents to offer personalized support, adjusting their level of involvement based on their child's needs and progress.

Empowering Independence: Gradually increasing the child's responsibility fosters independence and critical thinking skills, as they learn to apply concepts and solve problems on their own.

Social Cognitive Learning Theory

Key Principles

Observational Learning: Social cognitive learning theory, developed by Albert Bandura, emphasizes learning through observation and imitation. Children learn by watching others and imitating their actions, attitudes, and behaviors.

SelfEfficacy: This theory also highlights the importance of self efficacy, or the belief in one's ability to succeed, which can be influenced by positive experiences and encouragement from caregivers and teachers.

Application in Homeschooling

Modeling Behavior: As a child's primary caregiver and educator, parents model desired behaviors, problem solving strategies, and attitudes towards learning, directly impacting their child's learning and development.

Positive Support: By providing opportunities for observational learning and encouraging self efficacy, parents can help build their child's confidence and motivation to engage in learning.

Mirror Neurons and Learning

Understanding Mirror Neurons

Function: Mirror neurons are brain cells that activate both when a person performs an action and when they observe someone else performing that action. They play a role in understanding and imitating behaviors, emotions, and intentions.

Implications for Learning: Mirror neurons help children learn by observing and mimicking the actions and emotions of those around them, including their parents.

Application in Homeschooling

Interactive Learning: By actively participating in learning activities and demonstrating enthusiasm, parents engage their child's mirror neurons, facilitating imitation and understanding.

Emotional Connection: Displaying positive emotions and a growth mindset during learning activities helps children internalize these attitudes and approach challenges with a similar mindset.

Empowering Parents as Educators

Recognizing Your Role

Primary Influence: Parents are their child's first teachers, providing foundational experiences and shaping their attitudes towards learning and problem solving.

Active Engagement: By engaging in the gradual release of responsibility, modeling positive behaviors, and fostering observational learning, parents play a crucial role in their child's educational development.

Building Confidence

Ownership: Understanding that teaching is closely related to caregiving helps parents recognize the value of their role and the impact they have on their child's learning journey.

Empowerment: Embracing the principles of social cognitive learning theory and mirror neurons empowers parents to see themselves as effective educators who can foster a positive and enriching learning environment at home.

Creating a Humane Homeschool

Personalized Learning: In a humane homeschool, parents can tailor education to their child's unique needs, interests, and pace, ensuring a supportive and effective learning experience.

Holistic Development: By integrating principles of caregiving and education, parents can create a learning environment that nurtures not only academic skills but also emotional and social development.

In summary, teaching as an extension of caregiving, combined with an understanding of educational theories like the gradual release of responsibility, social cognitive learning, and mirror neurons, highlights the profound impact parents have as educators. By leveraging these concepts, parents can confidently create a humane homeschool that supports their child's holistic development and fosters a love of learning.

Creating your own curriculum

Research State or Local Standards

Access Standards: Obtain the state or local education standards for your child's grade level. These are often available on your state's department of education website or local school district websites.

Review Content Areas: Identify key learning goals for language arts, writing, reading, math, science, and social studies. Note the specific skills and knowledge expected at each grade level.

Interpret Standards for Your Curriculum

Break Down Standards: Translate broad standards into specific learning objectives and activities. For example, if the standard requires students to "understand multiplication," break this down into learning multiplication facts, solving word problems, and applying multiplication in real life contexts.

Developing the Curriculum

Language Arts

Reading: Include activities for phonics, vocabulary, comprehension, and fluency. Use diverse reading materials, including fiction and nonfiction.

Writing: Focus on grammar, sentence structure, and various forms of writing (narrative, expository, persuasive). Incorporate writing prompts and practice.

Spelling and Vocabulary: Integrate spelling lessons and vocabulary building exercises. Use word lists and contextual learning activities.

Math

Concepts and Skills: Cover basic arithmetic, number sense, place value, fractions, and problem solving. Use manipulatives and visual aids to support understanding.

Practice and Application: Provide exercises that apply math skills to real life situations. Include regular practice to reinforce concepts.

Science

Topics: Plan units on life science, physical science, earth science, and environmental science. Include hands-on experiments, observations, and investigations.

InquiryBased Learning: Encourage curiosity and exploration through inquiry based activities and scientific questioning.

Social Studies

Content: Cover history, geography, civics, and cultural studies. Include topics such as ancient civilizations, world cultures, and current events.

Critical Thinking: Use discussions, projects, and research to develop critical thinking and understanding of historical and social contexts.

Choosing Technology or a Hybrid Approach

TechnologyBased

Digital Resources: Utilize online educational platforms, apps, and software for interactive learning and practice.

Online Learning: Incorporate virtual classes, tutorials, and digital libraries for supplemental instruction.

NonTechnologyBased

Traditional Resources: Use textbooks, workbooks, and printed materials for instruction and practice.

HandsOn Activities: Focus on physical manipulatives, experiments, and real world applications without relying on screens.

Hybrid Approach

Balanced Use: Combine technology with traditional methods. For example, use online resources for interactive learning while relying on printed materials for practice and assessment.

Selective Integration: Choose technology tools that enhance learning and complement traditional methods rather than replace them.

Budgeting for Supplies

Create a Budget

Estimate Costs: Identify the costs associated with curriculum materials, technology, and supplies. Create a budget that includes both initial and ongoing expenses.

Track Spending: Keep track of expenditures and adjust the budget as needed to stay within financial limits.

Sourcing Materials

Thrift Stores: Look for educational materials, books, and supplies at thrift stores, garage sales, or secondhand shops. This can provide valuable resources at a lower cost.

Donations and Swaps: Seek donations from friends, family, or community groups. Consider swapping materials with other homeschooling families.

Using Existing Resources

Inventory Check: Review materials and resources you already have. Use existing textbooks, workbooks, and educational tools before purchasing new ones.

Repurposing: Repurposed materials creatively for new learning activities. For example, use old magazines for art projects or math games.

Researching and Including Field Trips

Identify Relevant Field Trips

Educational Value: Choose field trips that align with your curriculum and enhance learning. For example, visit a local museum, science center, historical site, or nature reserve.

Local Opportunities: Explore local resources and opportunities, such as community events, library programs, or nature walks.

Plan and Budget

Logistics: Plan field trip details, including transportation, admission fees, and necessary preparations.

Cost Management: Budget for field trip expenses and seek discounts, group rates, or free days at local attractions.

Valuing Under Consumption

Prioritize Existing Materials

Use What You Have: Maximize the use of existing resources before purchasing additional materials. This reduces waste and supports a sustainable approach to education.

Resource Sharing: Share materials with other homeschooling families or community groups to extend their use and reduce individual costs.

Mindful Purchasing

Evaluate Needs: Carefully evaluate the need for new materials and prioritize purchases that will have the most significant impact on learning.

EcoFriendly Options: Consider eco friendly and sustainable options when purchasing new materials.

Writing your own curriculum involves understanding and interpreting educational standards, developing a comprehensive plan for language arts, math, science, and social studies, and choosing between technology based, non technology based, or hybrid approaches. Budgeting carefully, sourcing materials wisely, and incorporating field trips can enhance your child's learning experience. By valuing existing resources and practicing under consumption, you create a more sustainable and mindful educational environment. With thoughtful planning and resourcefulness, you can develop a humane homeschool curriculum that supports your child's growth and aligns with your values.

Development of Language and Speech Sounds: From Birth to Adulthood

Birth to 6 Months: PreLinguistic Stage

Vocalization: Babies begin to coo and gurgle, producing vowel-like sounds.

Reflexive Crying: Different cries to signal needs (hunger, discomfort).

Listening: Recognize and respond to familiar voices, especially their mother's.

6 to 12 Months: Babbling Stage

Babbling: Combining consonants and vowels (e.g., "bababa," "dadada").

Phonetic Development: Experimenting with a variety of sounds, including those not in their native language.

First Words: Begin to understand simple words and may say their first word around 12 months.

12 to 18 Months: Early Words Stage

Single Words: Speaking single, often familiar words (e.g., "mama," "dada").

Naming: Using words to name objects and people.

Gestures: Using gestures along with speech to communicate.

18 to 24 Months: TwoWord Stage

Word Combinations: Combining two words to form simple sentences (e.g., "want cookie").

Vocabulary Explosion: Rapid increase in vocabulary.

Understanding: Comprehending more than they can express.

2 to 3 Years: Telegraphic Speech

Simple Sentences: Forming short sentences with essential words (e.g., "more juice").

Grammar Development: Beginning to use basic grammatical structures.

Pronunciation: Improving clarity of speech sounds but may still make errors.

3 to 5 Years: Early Childhood Stage

Complex Sentences: Using longer and more complex sentences.

Grammar and Syntax: Better understanding and use of grammar rules.

Articulation: Pronunciation becomes clearer, though some sounds may still be challenging (e.g., "r," "th").

5 to 7 Years: Refinement Stage

Speech Sounds: Mastering most speech sounds, though some may still develop.

Vocabulary and Syntax: Continued growth in vocabulary and more sophisticated sentence structures.

Storytelling: Ability to tell simple stories and follow more complex instructions.

7 to 12 Years: Later Childhood Stage

Fluency: Speech becomes more fluent and less effortful.

Complex Language: Use of complex and varied sentences, including passive voice and conditional clauses.

Pragmatics: Understanding and using language in different social contexts.

Adolescence to Adulthood: Advanced Language Stage

Abstract Thinking: Ability to discuss abstract concepts and hypothetical situations.

Sophisticated Vocabulary: Use of advanced and specialized vocabulary.

Refined Articulation: Clear and precise articulation of speech sounds.

Professional and Academic Language: Ability to switch between informal and formal language as appropriate.

Tips for Supporting Language Development

Talk and Read to Children: Engage in regular conversations and read aloud to promote vocabulary and comprehension.

Encourage Play: Provide opportunities for pretend play and storytelling to foster language use.

Model Good Speech: Speak clearly and correctly to model proper speech sounds and grammar.

Listen and Respond: Actively listen to children and respond to their attempts to communicate.

Provide Feedback: Gently correct mispronunciations and grammatical errors by modeling the correct form.

Encourage Interaction: Promote social interactions with peers to practice conversational skills.

Development of Phonemes by Age and Stage

Birth to 1 Year: PreLinguistic Stage

Reflexive Sounds: Crying, cooing, and other reflexive sounds.

Early Vocalization: Production of vowel-like sounds (e.g., "oo," "ah," "ee").

1 to 2 Years: Babbling and Early Words

Babbling: Repetition of simple consonant vowel combinations (e.g., "baba," "dada").

Early Words: First recognizable words often include easy phonemes like /m/, /n/, /b/, /d/, /p/, /t/.

2 to 3 Years: Expanding Phoneme Repertoire

Introduction of More Consonants:

/k/ as in "cat"

/g/ as in "go"

/f/ as in "fish"

/v/ as in "van"

Development of Vowel Sounds: Broadening use of long and short vowels (e.g., /i/ in "sit," /aɪ/ in "kite").

3 to 4 Years: Mastery of Simple Phonemes

More Consonants:

/s/ as in "sun"

/z/ as in "zoo"

/ʃ/ as in "shoe"

/ʧ/ as in "cheese"

/ʤ/ as in "juice"

Complex Vowel Combinations: Mastery of diphthongs (e.g., /eɪ/ in "cake," /aʊ/ in "cow").

4 to 5 Years: Refining Articulation

Tricky Consonants:

/r/ as in "run"

/l/ as in "lamp"

/θ/ as in "think"

/ð/ as in "this"

/ʒ/ as in "measure"

Consistent Use of Vowels: Consistent pronunciation of all vowel sounds, including /ʊ/ as in "book" and /ɔ:/ as in "saw".

5 to 6 Years: NearAdult Speech

Fluent Consonants: Mastery of remaining challenging consonants:

/ŋ/ as in "sing"

/h/ as in "hat"

/w/ as in "win"

/j/ as in "yes"

Full Vowel Repertoire: Complete and consistent use of vowel phonemes in various contexts.

6 to 7 Years: Polishing Speech

Speech Refinement: Minor adjustments and refinements in pronunciation.

Complex Consonant Blends: Mastery of consonant clusters (e.g., /str/ in "street," /spl/ in "splash").

Pronunciation Guide for the 44 Phonemes

Vowels (19 Phonemes)

Short Vowels:

/æ/ as in "cat"

/e/ as in "bed"

/ɪ/ as in "sit"

/ɒ/ as in "hot"

/ʌ/ as in "cup"

/ʊ/ as in "put"

Long Vowels:

/iː/ as in "feet"

/uː/ as in "moon"

/ɜː/ as in "bird"

/ɔː/ as in "saw"

/ɑː/ as in "car"

Diphthongs:

/eɪ/ as in "day"

/aɪ/ as in "eye"

/ɔɪ/ as in "boy"

/aʊ/ as in "now"

/əʊ/ as in "go"

/ɪə/ as in "ear"

/eə/ as in "air"

/ʊə/ as in "pure"

Consonants (25 Phonemes)

Plosives:

/p/ as in "pat"

/b/ as in "bat"

/t/ as in "tap"

/d/ as in "dog"

/k/ as in "cat"

/g/ as in "go"

Fricatives:

/f/ as in "fish"

/v/ as in "van"

/θ/ as in "think"

/ð/ as in "this"

/s/ as in "sun"

/z/ as in "zoo"

/ʃ/ as in "shoe"

/ʒ/ as in "measure"

/h/ as in "hat"

Affricates:

/tʃ/ as in "cheese"

/dʒ/ as in "juice"

Nasals:

/m/ as in "man"

/n/ as in "net"

/ŋ/ as in "sing"

Liquids:

/l/ as in "lamp"

/r/ as in "run"

Glides:

/w/ as in "win"

/j/ as in "yes"

Tips for Supporting Phoneme Development

Model Sounds: Clearly articulate phonemes during conversations and reading.

Interactive Reading: Use books with repetitive sounds and rhymes.

Games and Activities: Engage in activities that emphasize phoneme recognition (e.g., phoneme bingo).

Encourage Imitation: Have children repeat sounds and words.

Phoneme Isolation: Practice identifying and isolating individual phonemes in words.

Strategies for Developing and Modeling Phonemes at Home

Early Exposure to Sounds

Talk to Your Baby: Constantly talk to your baby using clear and simple language.

Sing Songs and Nursery Rhymes: These often contain repetitive sounds and rhythms that help babies recognize phonemes.

Reading Aloud

Daily Reading: Read books aloud to your child every day. Choose books with repetitive phrases and rhyming patterns.

Point and Pronounce: Point to objects in picture books and pronounce their names clearly.

Phonemic Awareness Activities

Sound Games: Play games that involve identifying and making sounds. For example, play "I Spy" with sounds ("I spy something that starts with /b/").

Rhyming Games: Engage in rhyming games and ask your child to think of words that rhyme.

Encouraging Imitation and Repetition

Model Sounds: Clearly articulate sounds and ask your child to repeat them.

Echo Game: Say a word or a sound, and have your child echo it back to you.

Practice Phoneme Isolation

Sound Identification: Ask your child to identify the first, middle, or last sound in a word (e.g., "What is the first sound in 'cat'?").

Sound Sorting: Sort objects or pictures based on their initial sounds.

Engaging in Structured Activities

Alphabet Books and Puzzles: Use alphabet books and puzzles to associate letters with their corresponding sounds.

Phonics Apps and Games: Utilize educational apps and games that focus on phonics and phonemic awareness.

Using Everyday Moments

Labeling Objects: Label household objects and emphasize their beginning sounds.

Sound Hunt: Go on a "sound hunt" around the house or neighborhood, looking for items that start with a particular sound.

Encouraging Writing and Drawing

Letter Writing: Encourage your child to write letters and simple words, emphasizing the sounds in each letter.

Drawing and Describing: Have your child draw pictures and describe them, focusing on clear pronunciation of sounds.

Examples of Activities by Phoneme Categories

Short Vowels

Games with Short Vowel Sounds: Create word lists with short vowel sounds (/æ/, /e/, /ɪ/, /ɒ/, /ʌ/, /ʊ/) and play matching or sorting games.

Long Vowels and Diphthongs

Flashcards with Long Vowel Words: Use flashcards with long vowel sounds (/iː/, /uː/, /ɜː/, /ɔː/, /ɑː/) and diphthongs (/eɪ/, /aɪ/, /ɔɪ/, /aʊ/, /əʊ/) to practice pronunciation.

Plosives and Fricatives

Sound Matching Games: Create or use existing games that match words starting with plosives (/p/, /b/, /t/, /d/, /k/, /g/) and fricatives (/f/, /v/, /θ/, /ð/, /s/, /z/, /ʃ/, /ʒ/, /h/).

Affricates and Nasals

Word Lists for Affricates and Nasals: Develop word lists for practicing affricates (/tʃ/, /dʒ/) and nasals (/m/, /n/, /ŋ/) and play word association games.

Liquids and Glides

Storytelling with Focus Sounds: Encourage your child to tell stories using words that emphasize liquids (/l/, /r/) and glides (/w/, /j/).

Tips for Parents

Be Patient and Positive: Celebrate small successes and be patient with challenges.

Make It Fun: Turn learning into a fun and engaging activity.

Be Consistent: Regular practice is key to phoneme development.

Provide a LanguageRich Environment: Surround your child with a variety of spoken and written language experiences.

Use Visual and Tactile Supports: Visual aids like letter cards and tactile activities like tracing letters in sand can reinforce phoneme learning.

By integrating these strategies into everyday interactions and activities, parents can effectively support their children's phoneme development, laying a strong foundation for reading and language skills.

Development of Reading Skills from Birth to Adulthood

Birth to Age 2: PreLiteracy Stage

Oracy: Babies and toddlers develop listening and speaking skills through interactions with caregivers. They learn to recognize and produce speech sounds, understand simple words, and follow basic instructions.

Vocabulary Building: Rapid growth in vocabulary as children learn new words daily.

Early Phonemic Awareness: Awareness of individual sounds in words starts to develop.

Ages 2 to 5: Emergent Literacy Stage

Phonemic Awareness: Recognizing and manipulating individual sounds in spoken words. Activities like rhyming and segmenting sounds become important.

Letter Recognition: Learning to identify letters and associate them with their corresponding sounds (alphabetic principle).

Oracy: Continued development of speaking and listening skills. Children start to tell simple stories and engage in conversations.

Vocabulary Expansion: Rapid vocabulary growth continues, supported by reading and conversation.

Early Writing: Experimenting with writing letters and simple words.

Ages 5 to 7: Early Reading Stage

Decoding Skills: Learning to sound out words by blending phonemes together. Mastery of simple CVC (consonantvowelconsonant) words.

Fluency: Beginning to read simple texts with some level of fluency. Repeated reading of familiar texts helps build fluency.

Grammar: Understanding basic sentence structures and beginning to use punctuation.

Orthography: Learning spelling patterns and rules. Beginning to recognize common sight words.

Oracy: Improved ability to express thoughts clearly and participate in discussions.

Morphology: Understanding the concept of root words and simple affixes (e.g., s for plurals).

Ages 7 to 9: Developing Reading Stage

Fluency: Reading with increased speed, accuracy, and expression. Developing the ability to read silently.

Comprehension: Beginning to understand and interpret more complex texts. Asking and answering questions about the text.

Grammar: Using more complex sentence structures and understanding grammatical rules.

Orthography: Spelling more complex words and understanding irregular spelling patterns.

Vocabulary: Continued expansion of vocabulary through reading and exposure to new words.

Morphology: Understanding more complex word structures, including prefixes and suffixes (e.g., un, re, ed, ing).

Ages 9 to 12: Transitional Reading Stage

Fluency: Reading fluently with good expression and comprehension. Ability to read a variety of texts, including fiction and nonfiction.

Comprehension: Developing critical thinking skills and the ability to summarize, infer, and draw conclusions from texts.

Grammar: Mastery of more complex grammatical structures. Understanding the function of different parts of speech.

Orthography: Mastery of most common spelling patterns and rules. Ability to use spelling strategies for unfamiliar words.

Vocabulary: Expanding vocabulary through independent reading and study of word origins and meanings.

Morphology: Understanding and using complex word forms and structures, including compound words and derivatives.

Ages 12 to 18: Adolescent Reading Stage

Fluency: Reading complex texts fluently and efficiently. Ability to read for different purposes (e.g., study, leisure).

Comprehension: Advanced comprehension skills, including analysis, synthesis, and evaluation of texts. Ability to understand and critique literary devices and themes.

Grammar: Mastery of complex and varied sentence structures. Understanding nuances in grammar and style.

Orthography: Mastery of spelling, including technical and specialized vocabulary.

Oracy: Ability to engage in sophisticated discussions and present arguments clearly and effectively.

Etymology: Understanding the origin and history of words, including Latin and Greek roots.

Morphology: Proficient use of morphology to understand and create complex words, including academic and technical vocabulary.

Adulthood: Advanced Reading Stage

Fluency: Reading with high proficiency, adapting reading strategies to different types of texts and purposes.

Comprehension: Deep understanding and critical analysis of complex texts. Ability to engage with advanced and specialized literature.

Grammar: Mastery of all grammatical rules and conventions. Ability to use grammar creatively and effectively in writing and speech.

Orthography: Complete mastery of spelling and ability to learn new, specialized terms as needed.

Oracy: Highly developed speaking and listening skills, capable of engaging in professional and academic discourse.

Etymology: Deep understanding of word origins, including the ability to deduce meanings of unfamiliar words based on their roots.

Morphology: Advanced use of morphological knowledge to understand and construct complex and technical vocabulary.

Tips for Supporting Reading Development at Home

Read Aloud Daily: Encourage a love for reading by reading aloud to children at every stage.

Provide a Rich Language Environment: Surround children with books, conversations, and opportunities to explore language.

Encourage Writing: Support children in writing stories, letters, and journals to develop their writing skills.

Play Word Games: Engage in games that promote phonemic awareness, vocabulary, and spelling.

Model Good Reading Habits: Show children that reading is valuable and enjoyable by being a reading role model.

Use Technology Wisely: Utilize educational apps and online resources that support reading development.

By understanding and supporting each stage of reading development, parents can help their children become proficient and confident readers, equipped with the skills needed for lifelong literacy and learning.

Development of Writing Skills from Birth to Adulthood

Birth to Age 2: PreWriting Stage

Oracy: Developing listening and speaking skills, which form the foundation for writing.

Fine Motor Skills: Developing the motor skills necessary for writing through activities like grasping objects, scribbling, and drawing.

Early Drawing: Experimenting with making marks on paper, which is the precursor to writing.

Ages 2 to 5: Emergent Writing Stage

Scribbling to Letter Formation: Transitioning from scribbling to forming recognizable letters and shapes.

Name Writing: Learning to write their own name and other familiar words.

Oracy and Writing Connection: Talking about their drawings and early writings to build the connection between spoken and written language.

Letter Recognition: Associating letters with their corresponding sounds and beginning to write simple words.

Early Orthography: Understanding that writing represents spoken language.

Ages 5 to 7: Early Writing Stage

Phonemic Awareness in Writing: Using knowledge of sounds to spell simple words phonetically.

Sentence Writing: Writing simple sentences, often with invented spelling.

Grammar: Beginning to understand and use basic punctuation (e.g., periods, capital letters).

Orthography: Recognizing and writing common sight words correctly.

Writing Fluency: Developing the ability to write more smoothly and with less effort.

Oracy: Using spoken language skills to dictate stories or sentences before writing them down.

Ages 7 to 9: Developing Writing Stage

Spelling Patterns: Learning and applying common spelling patterns and rules.

Grammar and Syntax: Using more complex sentences and understanding basic grammar rules (e.g., subject verb agreement, plurals).

Writing for Different Purposes: Writing narratives, descriptions, and simple informational texts.

Writing Fluency: Writing longer texts with greater ease and coherence.

Oracy: Using oral storytelling to enhance written narratives.

Ages 9 to 12: Transitional Writing Stage

Orthography: Mastering more complex spelling rules and irregular words.

Grammar: Using a variety of sentence structures and more advanced punctuation (e.g., commas, quotation marks).

Writing Process: Understanding and using the writing process (planning, drafting, revising, editing, and publishing).

Writing Fluency: Writing with greater speed and fluidity.

Morphology: Using prefixes, suffixes, and root words to understand and spell new words.

Vocabulary: Expanding vocabulary and using more precise words in writing.

Ages 12 to 18: Adolescent Writing Stage

Advanced Grammar and Syntax: Using complex and varied sentence structures, including compound and complex sentences.

Orthography: Consistent application of spelling rules and accurate spelling of advanced vocabulary.

Writing for Different Genres: Writing essays, reports, narratives, and creative pieces with clear structure and purpose.

Writing Fluency: Writing with confidence and clarity across different subjects and contexts.

Etymology and Morphology: Understanding the origins and structures of words to enhance vocabulary and spelling.

Critical Thinking in Writing: Developing arguments, analyzing texts, and synthesizing information in written form.

Adulthood: Advanced Writing Stage

Mastery of Grammar and Syntax: Using grammar and punctuation with precision and creativity.

Orthography: Accurate spelling of specialized and technical vocabulary.

Professional and Academic Writing: Writing effectively for various professional, academic, and personal purposes.

Writing Fluency: Writing effortlessly and adapting style to suit different audiences and purposes.

Etymology and Morphology: Using knowledge of word origins and structures to enrich writing.

Reflective and Analytical Writing: Engaging in reflective writing and advanced analysis in written form.

Tips for Supporting Writing Development at Home

Encourage Drawing and Scribbling: Provide ample opportunities for young children to draw and scribble as a foundation for writing.

Read Aloud and Discuss Books: Reading together and discussing stories can help children understand narrative structure and vocabulary.

Provide Writing Materials: Ensure children have access to paper, pencils, and other writing tools to practice writing.

Model Writing: Write notes, lists, and letters in front of children to show the practical uses of writing.

Engage in Writing Activities: Encourage writing through fun activities like writing stories, journals, or letters to family members.

Use Technology Wisely: Utilize educational apps and tools that support writing skills development.

Give Positive Feedback: Provide constructive feedback and celebrate successes in writing.

Connect Writing to Interests: Encourage children to write about topics they are passionate about to make writing more engaging.

Practice Writing Regularly: Set aside regular time for writing practice to build fluency and confidence.

Encourage Revision: Teach children the importance of revising and editing their work to improve clarity and correctness.

By understanding and supporting each stage of writing development, parents can help their children become proficient and confident writers, equipped with the skills needed for lifelong literacy and communication.

Development of Math Skills from Birth to Adulthood

Birth to Age 2: PreMath Skills

Number Sense: Recognizing quantities, differences in size, and basic counting (e.g., understanding "more" and "less").

Patterns and Sorting: Recognizing simple patterns and sorting objects by shape, color, or size.

Ages 2 to 5: Early Math Skills

Counting: Learning to count verbally, first to 10, then to 20 and beyond.

Number Recognition: Recognizing numerals and associating them with quantities.

Basic Arithmetic: Understanding simple addition and subtraction using objects or fingers.

Manipulatives: Using toys, blocks, and other objects to develop counting and basic arithmetic skills.

Measurement: Understanding concepts of size, weight, and length through play (e.g., comparing heights of toys).

Telling Time: Recognizing the basics of time (e.g., morning, afternoon, night).

Patterns: Creating and recognizing more complex patterns.

Ages 5 to 7: Early Elementary Math

Counting and Skip Counting: Counting by 2s, 5s, and 10s.

Number Lines: Using number lines to understand the sequence of numbers and basic arithmetic.

Place Value: Understanding the concept of tens and ones.

Basic Operations: Performing simple addition and subtraction problems.

Measurement: Using standard units to measure length, weight, and volume.

Telling Time: Learning to tell time to the nearest hour and half hour on analog clocks.

Data: Collecting and interpreting simple data (e.g., tally charts, basic bar graphs).

Fractions: Introduction to basic fractions (e.g., 1/2, 1/4) through visual aids and manipulatives.

Ages 7 to 9: Developing Math Skills

Advanced Arithmetic: Performing addition and subtraction with regrouping (carrying/borrowing).

Place Value: Understanding hundreds, tens, and ones.

Multiplication and Division: Learning basic multiplication and division facts.

Number Lines and Manipulatives: Using these tools for more complex problems.

Fractions: Understanding fractions as parts of a whole and using visual aids to compare fractions.

Measurement: Using rulers, scales, and measuring cups to understand length, weight, and volume.

Telling Time: Telling time to the nearest five minutes and understanding elapsed time.

Data: Collecting, organizing, and interpreting data using bar graphs and pictographs.

Ages 9 to 12: Upper Elementary Math

Multiplication and Division: Mastering multiplication tables and long division.

Place Value: Understanding place value up to millions.

Fractions and Decimals: Converting between fractions and decimals, performing operations with fractions.

Measurement: Understanding and using different units of measurement, including metric units.

Telling Time: Calculating elapsed time and understanding schedules.

Data: Interpreting more complex data sets and creating graphs (e.g., line graphs, pie charts).

Geometry: Understanding basic geometric shapes and properties.

Ages 12 to 18: Middle and High School Math

Algebra: Introduction to algebraic concepts, solving equations, and understanding functions.

Geometry: Understanding properties of shapes, theorems, and proofs.

Advanced Arithmetic: Performing operations with larger numbers, fractions, decimals, and percentages.

Measurement: Applying measurement in various contexts, including geometry and science.

Data Analysis: Interpreting and analyzing data sets, understanding probability and statistics.

Advanced Topics: Exploring more complex topics like trigonometry, calculus, and advanced algebra.

Adulthood: Advanced Math Skills

Application of Math: Using math skills in daily life, work, and further education.

Continued Learning: Engaging in lifelong learning of math for personal and professional development.

Specialized Math: Applying specialized mathematical knowledge in fields such as engineering, economics, or computer science.

Tips for Parents to Support Math Development at Home

PreMath Skills (Birth to Age 2)

Talk About Numbers: Count objects during play, meals, or while reading books.

Encourage Exploration: Provide toys that can be stacked, sorted, and compared.

Play Simple Games: Engage in games that involve counting, sorting, and identifying shapes.

Early Math Skills (Ages 2 to 5)

Counting Games: Use everyday activities to practice counting (e.g., counting steps, toys).

Use Manipulatives: Provide objects like blocks or beads for counting and simple arithmetic.

Storytime: Read books that incorporate counting, patterns, and basic math concepts.

Measure and Compare: Use measuring cups, scales, and rulers during cooking or play.

Early Elementary Math (Ages 5 to 7)

Number Lines: Use number lines for visual understanding of addition and subtraction.

Skip Counting: Practice counting by 2s, 5s, and 10s through songs and games.

Telling Time: Use analog clocks and time telling games.

Play Math Games: Use board games and card games that involve math skills.

Developing Math Skills (Ages 7 to 9)

Practice Multiplication: Use flashcards and multiplication games.

Fractions with Food: Cut food into fractions to visually demonstrate parts of a whole.

Measurement Activities: Engage in activities that involve measuring (e.g., baking, DIY projects).

Data Collection: Collect and graph data on everyday topics (e.g., favorite fruits, daily temperatures).

Upper Elementary Math (Ages 9 to 12)

Math in Daily Life: Involve children in budgeting, shopping, and cooking to apply math skills.

Geometry Games: Use games and puzzles to explore geometric concepts.

Use Technology: Utilize educational apps and websites that reinforce math skills.

Encourage ProblemSolving: Provide puzzles and challenges that require critical thinking.

Middle and High School Math (Ages 12 to 18)

Homework Help: Provide support and resources for homework and study.

RealWorld Applications: Show how math is used in various careers and everyday tasks.

Advanced Resources: Encourage the use of online courses, math clubs, and tutoring for advanced topics.

Encourage Exploration: Support interests in math related fields like computer science, engineering, or finance.

By understanding the stages of math development and using these strategies, parents can effectively support their children's math learning at home, laying a strong foundation for future academic and personal success.

Strategies for Encouraging Math Confidence

Create a Positive Math Environment

Avoid Negative Talk: Be mindful of how you talk about math. Avoid saying things like "I'm not good at math" as it can create a negative mindset.

Encourage a Growth Mindset: Emphasize that math skills can be developed with practice and effort. Praise effort, persistence, and strategies rather than innate ability.

Incorporate Math into Daily Life

RealLife Applications: Show how math is used in everyday activities like cooking, shopping, budgeting, and DIY projects. This makes math relevant and practical.

Math Games: Play board games, card games, and puzzles that involve math skills. This makes learning fun and interactive.

Provide the Right Tools and Resources

Manipulatives: Use objects like blocks, beads, and counters to make abstract concepts concrete.

Technology: Utilize educational apps, websites, and online games that make learning math engaging and interactive.

Offer Support and Encouragement

Be Available: Help with homework and be available to answer questions. Show patience and provide guidance without doing the work for them.

Celebrate Successes: Celebrate achievements, no matter how small. This builds a sense of accomplishment and motivates further effort.

Build a Strong Foundation

Focus on Basics: Ensure your child has a strong grasp of basic math concepts before moving on to more complex topics.

Practice Regularly: Encourage regular practice to reinforce skills and build confidence through repetition.

Use Social Cognitive Learning Theory Principles

Modeling: Demonstrate math related tasks and problem solving strategies. Children learn by observing others, especially their parents.

SelfEfficacy: Help your child develop belief in their own abilities by setting achievable goals and providing opportunities for success.

Social Interactions: Encourage group activities and discussions where children can share strategies and solutions.

Encourage ProblemSolving and Critical Thinking

Ask OpenEnded Questions: Encourage your child to explain their thinking and reasoning. This promotes deeper understanding and confidence in their problem solving abilities.

Encourage Exploration: Allow your child to explore different methods and solutions. This fosters creativity and confidence in their ability to tackle problems.

Model Positive Attitudes Toward Math

Show Enthusiasm: Show enthusiasm for math and its applications. Your positive attitude can be contagious.

Share Your Own Learning: If you're learning something new related to math, share your experiences and struggles. This normalizes the learning process and shows that it's okay to make mistakes.

Provide Opportunities for Success

Differentiated Learning: Tailor math activities to your child's level and interests. This ensures they are challenged but not overwhelmed.

Incremental Challenges: Gradually increase the difficulty of math problems as your child's skills improve. This helps them build confidence step by step.

Encourage a Supportive Community

Study Groups: Encourage your child to study with peers. Collaborative learning can boost confidence and provide additional support.

Tutoring: If needed, consider hiring a tutor who can provide personalized instruction and encouragement.

Practical Examples for Encouraging Math Confidence

For Younger Children (Ages 27)

Counting Games: Play games that involve counting objects, such as counting toys during cleanup.

Simple Addition and Subtraction: Use snacks or toys to demonstrate basic addition and subtraction.

Shape Hunts: Go on a shape hunt around the house or neighborhood to identify different shapes.

For Older Children (Ages 712)

Cooking Together: Follow recipes that involve measuring ingredients and calculating proportions.

Shopping Challenges: Give them a budget and have them help with grocery shopping, comparing prices, and calculating totals.

Building Projects: Engage in building projects that require measuring and planning, such as constructing a birdhouse.

For Adolescents (Ages 1218)

Budgeting: Help them create a personal budget, track expenses, and understand financial planning.

STEM Activities: Encourage participation in STEMrelated clubs or activities that involve math.

Math Competitions: Encourage involvement in math competitions or clubs to challenge their skills and build confidence.

By applying Social Cognitive Learning Theory principles, parents can create a supportive and encouraging environment that fosters math confidence and helps children develop a positive attitude toward math. This approach emphasizes the importance of modeling, social interactions, and building self efficacy, all of which contribute to a child's success in math.

Development of Science Skills from Birth to Adulthood

Birth to Age 2: Early Science Exploration

Sensory Exploration: Engage in activities that stimulate the senses, such as exploring textures, sounds, and smells.

Observation: Encourage observation of the natural world, such as watching animals, plants, and weather changes.

Cause and Effect: Explore simple cause and effect relationships (e.g., dropping a toy to see it fall).

Ages 2 to 5: Foundational Science Skills

InquiryBased Learning: Encourage curiosity by asking questions about how things work and why things happen.

Nature Play: Explore natural environments through activities like nature walks, gardening, and playing with natural materials.

Basic Concepts: Introduce basic concepts of living and nonliving things, and simple ecosystems (e.g., plants need water to grow).

Ages 5 to 7: Early Elementary Science

Observation Skills: Develop skills in observing and describing natural phenomena (e.g., different types of plants and animals).

Simple Experiments: Conduct basic science experiments to explore concepts like plant growth, weather patterns, and animal behaviors.

Biodiversity Awareness: Introduce the concept of biodiversity by identifying and learning about different species in local environments.

Ages 7 to 9: Developing Science Understanding

Scientific Method: Begin to understand and apply the scientific method (e.g., asking questions, making predictions, conducting experiments).

Environmental Impact: Discuss the impact of human activities on the environment (e.g., pollution, deforestation).

Biodiversity Projects: Participate in projects that involve cataloging local wildlife or planting a garden to support local species.

Ages 9 to 12: Upper Elementary Science

Ecological Systems: Explore more complex ecological systems and the interdependence of organisms within these systems.

Environmental Conservation: Learn about conservation efforts and the importance of protecting natural habitats.

Data Collection: Engage in collecting and analyzing data related to environmental science (e.g., tracking weather patterns, measuring plant growth).

Ages 12 to 18: Middle and High School Science

Advanced Topics: Study more advanced topics in biodiversity, environmental science, and physical science (e.g., ecosystems, climate change, renewable energy).

Ethical Considerations: Discuss ethical issues related to environmental science, such as sustainability, conservation ethics, and human impacts on ecosystems.

Research Projects: Conduct independent or group research projects on topics like endangered species, habitat restoration, or environmental policies.

Adulthood: Advanced Science Skills

Applied Science: Apply scientific knowledge to real world problems, including careers in environmental science, biology, and conservation.

Lifelong Learning: Engage in ongoing learning about scientific advancements, environmental issues, and ethical considerations.

Advocacy: Participate in advocacy for environmental conservation, sustainability practices, and biodiversity protection.

Tips for Encouraging Science Confidence

Create a Positive Science Environment

Model Curiosity: Show enthusiasm for science and environmental topics. Share your curiosity and interest in the natural world with your child.

Encourage Inquiry: Foster a culture of questioning and exploration. Validate their questions and encourage them to seek answers.

Incorporate Science into Daily Life

RealWorld Applications: Relate science concepts to everyday activities (e.g., cooking to understand chemical reactions, gardening to learn about plant biology).

Nature Exploration: Spend time outdoors observing wildlife, plants, and ecosystems. Discuss biodiversity and environmental impact.

Provide the Right Tools and Resources

Science Kits and Books: Use science kits, books, and educational resources that focus on biodiversity, environmental science, and ethical practices.

Technology: Utilize educational apps and websites to explore interactive science content and virtual field trips.

Offer Support and Encouragement

Be Available: Help with science projects and provide guidance for research and experiments. Show interest and provide encouragement.

Celebrate Successes: Acknowledge and celebrate achievements in science, whether big or small, to build confidence.

Build a Strong Foundation

Focus on Basics: Ensure a solid understanding of basic science concepts before moving on to more complex topics.

Encourage Regular Practice: Reinforce science learning through regular activities and discussions.

Use Social Cognitive Learning Theory Principles

Modeling: Demonstrate scientific processes and ethical behavior in your own actions. Children learn by observing and imitating.

SelfEfficacy: Help your child develop confidence in their scientific abilities by providing achievable goals and positive feedback.

Social Interactions: Encourage participation in group activities, science clubs, or environmental organizations where they can share knowledge and learn from others.

Encourage ProblemSolving and Critical Thinking

Ask OpenEnded Questions: Encourage your child to think critically about scientific phenomena and environmental issues by asking open-ended questions.

Encourage Exploration: Allow your child to explore various scientific methods and solutions. This promotes creativity and problem solving skills.

Model Positive Attitudes Toward Science

Show Enthusiasm: Express excitement and curiosity about scientific discoveries and environmental issues.

Share Learning Experiences: Discuss your own scientific learning and experiences, highlighting the importance of ongoing inquiry and ethical considerations.

Provide Opportunities for Success

Differentiated Learning: Tailor science activities and projects to your child's interests and skill level. This helps maintain engagement and confidence.

Incremental Challenges: Gradually introduce more complex scientific concepts and projects as their skills improve.

Encourage a Supportive Community

Study Groups: Encourage participation in science clubs or study groups to foster collaboration and mutual support.

Community Involvement: Engage in community science projects or environmental initiatives to provide real world application and advocacy experience.

By incorporating these strategies, parents can support their children's development in science, particularly in biodiversity and environmental science, while fostering confidence and ethical understanding through Social Cognitive Learning Theory principles.

General K12 Science Curriculum Overview

Early Childhood (Ages 35)

Exploration and Observation

Standards: PreK standards.

Topics:

Sensory exploration (textures, sounds, smells).

Simple observations of natural phenomena (e.g., weather changes, plant growth).

Activities:

Nature walks to observe plants and animals.

Sensory bins with natural materials (sand, water, leaves).

Basic Concepts of Living Things

Standards: PreK standards.

Topics:

Identifying living vs. nonliving things.

Basic needs of plants and animals.

Activities:

Growing plants from seeds and observing their growth.

Sorting activities with pictures of animals and plants.

Grades K2 (Ages 58)

Introduction to Ecosystems and Biology

Standards: K2 standards.

Topics:

Basic ecosystems and habitats (e.g., forests, oceans).

Simple food chains and webs.

Introduction to basic biology (e.g., body parts, senses).

Activities:

Building a model of a simple ecosystem.

Creating food chain diagrams with local animals and plants.

Introduction to Chemistry Concepts

Standards: K2 standards.

Topics:

Basic concepts of matter (solids, liquids, gasses).

Simple physical changes (e.g., melting, freezing).

Activities:

Mix baking soda and vinegar to observe reactions.

Exploring water states through freezing and melting.

Environmental Impact and Conservation

Standards: K2 standards.

Topics:

Human impact on the environment (e.g., pollution).

Basic conservation efforts (e.g., recycling).

Activities:

Recycling projects and discussions on reducing waste.

Nature cleanup activities.

Grades 35 (Ages 811)

Biodiversity and Biology

Standards: 35 standards.

Topics:

Diversity of living organisms and their adaptations.

Basic anatomy and functions of plants and animals.

Activities:

Creating a biodiversity poster with different species.

Research projects on animal adaptations and habitats.

Basic Chemistry

Standards: 35 standards.

Topics:

Properties of materials (e.g., texture, color, flexibility).

Introduction to chemical reactions (e.g., combining substances).

Activities:

Experiments to observe physical and chemical changes (e.g., mixing substances).

Simple chemical reactions using household items.

Environmental Systems and Conservation

Standards: 35 standards.

Topics:

Ecosystem interactions and energy flow.

Importance of conservation and protecting natural resources.

Activities:

Experiments to understand ecosystems (e.g., terrariums).

Community projects for local environmental conservation.

Grades 68 (Ages 1114)

Advanced Biology and Ecology

Standards: MS standards.

Topics:

Detailed study of ecosystems, biomes, and biodiversity.

Introduction to genetics and cellular biology.

Activities:

Field studies and data collection on local biodiversity.

Genetics projects and lab experiments.

Chemistry and Chemical Reactions

Standards: MS standards.

Topics:

Atoms and molecules.

Chemical reactions and equations.

States of matter and changes.

Activities:

Laboratory experiments to study reactions and compounds.

Creating models of molecules and chemical structures.

Environmental Science and Ethical Considerations

Standards: MS standards.

Topics:

Human impact on ecosystems (e.g., climate change, deforestation).

Ethical considerations in environmental science (e.g., sustainability).

Activities:

Debates or discussions on environmental issues and solutions.

Projects on renewable energy sources and sustainability practices.

Grades 912 (Ages 1418)

Advanced Biology

Standards: HS standards.

Topics:

Advanced topics in genetics, evolution, and physiology.

Ecological interactions and conservation biology.

Activities:

Research projects on genetic traits or conservation efforts.

Laboratory experiments on physiological processes and ecological studies.

Advanced Chemistry

Standards: HS standards.

Topics:

Chemical bonding and reactions.

Organic chemistry and biochemistry.

Thermodynamics and kinetics.

Activities:

Conducting experiments to understand chemical reactions and properties.

Investigating organic compounds and their reactions.

Environmental Science and Policy

Standards: HS standards.

Topics:

In Depth study of environmental issues (e.g., global warming, resource management).

Analysis of environmental policies and their impact.

Activities:

Research and presentations on current environmental issues and policies.

Advocacy projects and involvement in local environmental initiatives.

Ethics and Sustainable Practices

Standards: HS standards.

Topics:

Ethical implications of scientific research and technology.

Sustainable practices and their role in environmental conservation.

Activities:

Debates on ethical issues in science and technology.

Projects on sustainable practices and their implementation.

Tips for Integrating Social Cognitive Learning Theory

Modeling and Observation

Demonstrate Inquiry: Show curiosity and engage in scientific exploration and discussions.

Share Experiences: Talk about your own experiences with science, chemistry, and biology.

Encouraging SelfEfficacy

Set Achievable Goals: Help students set and achieve scientific goals.

Support Independent Learning: Encourage students to pursue their own research interests and projects.

Social Interactions

Group Projects: Facilitate group work and collaborative projects to build teamwork and communication skills.

Community Involvement: Encourage participation in community science and environmental projects.

Critical Thinking and Problem Solving

Ask OpenEnded Questions: Foster critical thinking by asking questions that require thoughtful answers.

Explore Different Solutions: Encourage experimentation and exploration of various scientific methods and solutions.

This detailed curriculum offers a comprehensive approach to science education from early childhood through high school, including biodiversity, environmental science, chemistry, and biology. It incorporates Social Cognitive Learning Theory principles to support science confidence and engagement.

General History Curriculum Breakdown

Early Childhood (Ages 35)

Introduction to Community and Social Interaction

Standards: PreK standards.

Topics:

Understanding community roles (e.g., family, friends, helpers).

Basic concepts of rules and cooperation.

Activities:

Roleplaying community helpers.

Reading simple stories about different communities and cultures.

Exploration of Stories and Traditions

Standards: PreK standards.

Topics:

Introduction to simple folktales and fables.

Exploring different cultures through stories.

Activities:

Reading and discussing simple fables and fairy tales.

Creating their own stories with moral lessons.

Grades K2 (Ages 58)

Introduction to Historical Concepts

Standards: K2 standards.

Topics:

Understanding the concept of time (past, present, future).

Basic history of early communities and ancient civilizations.

Activities:

Creating timelines of their own lives.

Learning about early communities through storytelling and crafts.

Early Civilizations and Creation Myths

Standards: K2 standards.

Topics:

Introduction to creation myths of early civilizations (e.g., Sumerians, Greeks, Romans).

Understanding the role of stories in explaining the world.

Activities:

Reading simplified versions of creation myths.

Drawing or acting out key elements of these myths.

Introduction to Social Studies and Civics

Standards: K2 standards.

Topics:

Basic concepts of rules and responsibilities.

Introduction to family, community, and simple civic concepts.

Activities:

Discussing family roles and rules.

Creating a class "community" with rules and roles.

Grades 35 (Ages 811)

Exploring Early Civilizations and Fables

Standards: 35 standards.

Topics:

Detailed study of early civilizations (e.g., Sumerians, Egyptians, Greeks, Romans).

Use of fables and myths to explain complex ideas (e.g., Aesop's Fables).

Activities:

Reading and analyzing ancient fables and myths.

Creating their own fables to address modern issues.

Introduction to Civics and Government

Standards: 35 standards.

Topics:

Basic principles of government and civic responsibilities.

Understanding community roles and the importance of rules.

Activities:

Roleplaying different government roles.

Creating simple government structures and learning about their functions.

Media Literacy Basics

Standards: 35 standards.

Topics:

Understanding the role of media in society.

Basic skills in identifying different types of media (e.g., books, TV, internet).

Activities:

Comparing different types of media and their purposes.

Creating simple media projects (e.g., news reports, advertisements).

Grades 68 (Ages 1114)

InDepth Study of Ancient Civilizations and Their Stories

Standards: MS standards.

Topics:

Detailed exploration of ancient civilizations (e.g., Mesopotamia, Greece, Rome).

Analyzing how fables and myths were used to teach lessons and explain phenomena.

Activities:

Research projects on ancient myths and their cultural significance.

Writing essays on the role of fables in ancient societies.

Foundations of Civics and Government

Standards: MS standards.

Topics:

Study of democratic principles and historical government structures.

Understanding the role of citizens and civic engagement.

Activities:

Debates on historical and contemporary civic issues.

Simulating government processes (e.g., mock elections).

Media Literacy and Critical Thinking

Standards: MS standards.

Topics:

Advanced media literacy skills (e.g., evaluating sources, understanding bias).

Analyzing the impact of media on society and individuals.

Activities:

Critiquing news articles and media reports.

Creating media projects that address societal issues.

Grades 912 (Ages 1418)

Advanced Study of World History and Creation Myths

Standards: HS standards.

Topics:

In Depth exploration of major civilizations and their contributions (e.g., Mesopotamia, Grecce, Rome).

Analyzing the role of creation myths and fables in understanding human experience.

Activities:

Research papers on the influence of myths on ancient cultures.

Comparative studies of creation myths from different civilizations.

Civics, Government, and Ethical Considerations

Standards: HS standards.

Topics:

Detailed study of modern governments, political systems, and civic responsibilities.

Exploration of ethical issues in governance and citizenship.

Activities:

Case studies on political systems and their impact on society.

Debates on ethical issues in contemporary governance.

Advanced Media Literacy and Analysis

Standards: HS standards.

Topics:

Advanced skills in media analysis and evaluation.

Understanding media influence and its role in shaping public opinion.

Activities:

Creating multimedia projects that analyze media trends.

Evaluating the impact of media on societal issues.

Tips for Ethical and Humane Homeschooling

Foster Critical Thinking

Encourage Inquiry: Promote questions and discussions about historical events, government systems, and media.

Analyze Fables and Myths: Discuss how fables and myths were used to convey lessons and address complex topics.

Promote Inclusivity and Diversity

Inclusive Curriculum: Ensure that the study of history and social studies includes diverse perspectives and voices.

Ethical Discussions: Address ethical issues with sensitivity and respect for different viewpoints.

Model Ethical Behavior

Demonstrate Values: Model values such as empathy, respect, and ethical decision making in discussions and activities.

Encourage Social Responsibility: Engage in community service and civic activities to reinforce the importance of social responsibility.

Encourage Media Literacy

Evaluate Sources: Teach students to critically evaluate media sources and understand bias.

Promote Responsible Media Use: Encourage responsible use of media and technology in a digital age.

This curriculum provides a comprehensive framework for teaching social studies, civics, media literacy, and human history, from early childhood through high school, with an emphasis on ethical and humane homeschooling practices. It integrates the study of ancient civilizations, creation myths, and the role of fables in critical thinking, while also addressing modern civic and media literacy skills.

Creation Myths and Fables

Early Childhood (Ages 35)

Introduction to Stories and Morals

Standards: PreK standards.

Topics:

Basic elements of stories (characters, settings, and morals).

Simple, age appropriate creation myths and fables.

Activities:

Reading simplified versions of creation myths and fables with illustrations.

Discussing the morals and basic ideas behind these stories.

Exploration of Community Values

Standards: PreK standards.

Topics:

Introduction to concepts of community and shared values through stories.

Activities:

Comparing values from different creation myths and fables.

Roleplaying scenarios from the stories to understand their lessons.

Grades K2 (Ages 58)

Foundations of Stories and Cultures

Standards: K2 standards.

Topics:

Basic understanding of creation myths and their role in explaining the world.

Introduction to various fables from different cultures.

Activities:

Reading and discussing creation myths from Sumer, India, China, Greece, Africa, North America, and South America.

Drawing and retelling simplified versions of these stories.

Connecting Stories to Cultural Values

Standards: K2 standards.

Topics:

Understanding how creation myths and fables reflect cultural beliefs and values.

Activities:

Comparing the morals of fables with the explanations provided in creation myths.

Discussing how these stories teach about community values and responsibilities.

Understanding Community Roles and Responsibilities

Standards: K2 standards.

Topics:

Exploration of social roles and responsibilities depicted in myths and fables.

Activities:

Roleplaying characters from creation myths and fables.

Discussing different social roles and how they are portrayed in stories.

Grades 35 (Ages 811)

InDepth Study of Creation Myths

Standards: 35 standards.

Topics:

Detailed exploration of creation myths from various cultures:

Sumer: The Enuma Elish (creation from chaos, the rise of gods).

India: The Rigveda (creation from the cosmic ocean, the god Vishnu).

China: The Pangu myth (creation of the world from the cosmic egg).

Greece: The Theogony by Hesiod (creation of gods and the universe).

Africa: The Yoruba creation myth (creation by the deity Olodumare).

North America: Iroquois creation myth (creation of the world from the Sky World).

South America: Inca creation myth (the creation by Viracocha).

Activities:

Research projects on each creation myth and its cultural significance.

Creating visual timelines and maps to illustrate the stories.

Connecting Myths to Historical and Cultural Contexts

Standards: 35 standards.

Topics:

How creation myths relate to the historical and cultural contexts of their societies.

Activities:

Writing essays on how creation myths reflect societal values and beliefs.

Comparing and contrasting creation myths from different cultures.

Exploring Civic Values Through Stories

Standards: 35 standards.

Topics:

Introduction to civic values and responsibilities depicted in myths and fables.

Activities:

Creating guides on civic virtues based on lessons from creation myths and fables.

Roleplaying civic scenarios inspired by stories.

Grades 68 (Ages 1114)

Advanced Study of Creation Myths

Standards: MS standards.

Topics:

Comparative analysis of creation myths from different cultures.

Understanding the role of myths in shaping cultural identity and values.

Activities:

Researching and presenting on the similarities and differences among creation myths.

Analyzing how myths have influenced historical and cultural narratives.

Analyzing Ethical and Social Themes

Standards: MS standards.

Topics:

Examination of ethical and social themes presented in creation myths and fables.

Activities:

Debating the ethical implications of various myths.

Comparing how different cultures address similar themes and social issues.

Media Literacy and Historical Reflection

Standards: MS standards.

Topics:

Analyzing the portrayal of creation myths and fables in various media.

Activities:

Creating multimedia projects that explore the impact of myths and fables on modern culture.

Analyzing how contemporary media represents ancient stories.

Grades 912 (Ages 1418)

InDepth Historical and Cultural Analysis

Standards: HS standards.

Topics:

Detailed analysis of creation myths and their role in ancient civilizations.

Comparative studies of myths from Sumer, India, China, Greece, Africa, North America, and South America.

Activities:

Writing research papers on the historical significance of creation myths.

Analyzing how myths have shaped cultural and historical narratives.

Critical Examination of Themes and Lessons

Standards: HS standards.

Topics:

Analysis of moral, ethical, and philosophical themes in creation myths and fables.

Activities:

Writing analytical essays on the lessons and values presented in creation myths.

Debating the relevance of these themes in contemporary society.

Advanced Media Literacy and Reflection

Standards: HS standards.

Topics:

Exploring how the media influences the interpretation of creation myths and fables.

Activities:

Creating documentary style projects on the influence of creation myths across cultures.

Analyzing modern adaptations and representations of ancient stories.

Tips for Teaching Creation Myths and Fables

Use Comparative Analysis

Compare Stories: Analyze similarities and differences between creation myths from various cultures and how they explain the origins of the world.

Encourage Critical Thinking

Discuss Themes: Explore the ethical, social, and philosophical themes in creation myths and fables and their relevance to contemporary issues.

Integrate Various Media

Utilize Diverse Resources: Use books, films, art, and digital resources to explore and compare creation myths and fables.

Foster Cultural Appreciation

Highlight Cultural Contexts: Emphasize the cultural contexts and values reflected in each creation myth and fable to provide a deeper understanding of diverse perspectives.

Creation Myths and Anthropology

Anthropological Perspective

Understanding Cultural Context: Anthropology studies human societies and cultures, and creation myths offer insight into how ancient cultures explained their origins and the nature of existence. These myths often reflect the values, social structures, and environmental interactions of the cultures from which they originated.

Rituals and Practices: Creation myths are often tied to rituals and practices that shape the identity and social organization of a community. For example, myths might influence seasonal festivals, religious ceremonies, or social norms.

Cultural Comparison: Anthropologists compare creation myths across cultures to understand common themes, such as creation from chaos, divine beings, or the relationship between humans and nature. This comparative analysis helps highlight both universal human concerns and unique cultural expressions.

Application to Today:

Cultural Preservation: Understanding creation myths helps preserve and appreciate the cultural heritage of various societies. It also informs contemporary cultural practices and identity.

Cultural Sensitivity: Awareness of different creation myths fosters respect and sensitivity toward diverse cultural beliefs and practices in a globalized world.

Creation Myths and Mythology

Mythological Perspective

Symbolism and Archetypes: Mythology explores the symbolic meanings and archetypes present in creation myths. These myths often use symbolic language to convey fundamental truths about existence, morality, and human nature. For instance, creation from chaos or a cosmic battle often symbolizes the establishment of order and stability.

Narrative Structures: Myths often follow specific narrative structures, such as the emergence of the world from primordial chaos or the actions of deities to shape the cosmos. Analyzing these structures helps understand how different cultures conceptualize the universe and human existence.

Application to Today:

Influence on Literature and Art: Mythological themes from creation myths continue to influence literature, art, and popular culture. Understanding these myths enhances the interpretation of modern works that draw on ancient symbols and narratives.

Psychological Insights: Creation myths provide insights into collective human psychology and shared human experiences, helping us understand the psychological and emotional aspects of mythmaking.

Creation Myths and Philosophy

Philosophical Perspective

Ontology and Metaphysics: Creation myths address fundamental questions about the nature of existence, reality, and the origins of the universe. Philosophers examine these myths to explore concepts such as being, existence, and the nature of the divine.

Ethics and Morality: Many creation myths contain implicit moral lessons or ethical guidelines. Philosophers analyze these to understand how ancient cultures conceptualized morality and ethical behavior.

Application to Today:

Existential Reflection: Philosophical exploration of creation myths can provide contemporary individuals with insights into existential questions and the search for meaning in life.

Ethical Frameworks: Analyzing the moral lessons from creation myths can contribute to discussions about ethics and morality in modern contexts.

Creation Myths and Religion

Religious Perspective

Sacred Texts and Beliefs: Creation myths are often foundational to religious traditions, providing explanations for the origins of the world and the role of deities or divine beings. They are central to the sacred texts and doctrines of many religions.

Rituals and Worship: Creation myths often inform religious rituals, ceremonies, and worship practices. They provide a basis for understanding divine actions and the relationship between the divine and the human.

Application to Today:

Interfaith Dialogue: Understanding creation myths from various religions promotes interfaith dialogue and respect for different religious beliefs and practices.

Religious Identity: Creation myths play a crucial role in shaping religious identity and practices. Recognizing their significance helps in understanding the diversity of religious expressions and beliefs.

Integrating Creation Myths into Education and Contemporary Understanding

Cultural Literacy:

Educational Programs: Incorporating the study of creation myths into educational programs helps students gain a broader understanding of human history, cultural diversity, and religious traditions.

Critical Thinking:

Analytical Skills: Analyzing creation myths encourages critical thinking and helps students understand how stories shape and reflect human experiences and values.

Ethical and Philosophical Inquiry:

Moral Lessons: Exploring the ethical and philosophical dimensions of creation myths fosters a deeper understanding of human values and existential questions.

Cultural Appreciation:

Global Perspective: Studying creation myths from various cultures enhances global awareness and appreciation for the diversity of human thought and belief.

By examining creation myths through the lenses of anthropology, mythology, philosophy, and religion, students and individuals can gain a richer and more nuanced understanding of how different cultures and belief systems address fundamental questions about existence, morality, and the nature of the universe.

Incorporating diverse perspectives into a humane homeschool curriculum and encouraging critical thinking skills can enrich students' understanding of myths, culture, and religion as interconnected elements of collective human history.

Integrating Diverse Perspectives

Cultural Diversity and Mythology

Exposure to Various Myths: By including creation myths and cultural stories from a variety of societies (e.g., Sumerian, Indian, Chinese, Greek, African, Native American, South American), students gain insight into different ways cultures explain the origins of the world and humanity.

Understanding Shared Themes: Exploring common themes (e.g., creation from chaos, divine intervention) across diverse myths helps students see universal aspects of human experience while appreciating unique cultural expressions.

Cultural Relativity and Religion

Comparative Religion Studies: Introducing students to different religious beliefs and practices helps them understand how various cultures conceptualize the divine, moral principles, and the human role in the universe.

Respect for Diversity: Emphasizing respect for diverse religious perspectives encourages students to appreciate the richness of global religious traditions and fosters empathy towards differing beliefs.

Historical and Social Context

Historical Influences: Discussing how historical events and social structures influence myths and religious beliefs helps students understand the context in which these narratives emerged.

Cultural Evolution: Examining how myths and religious practices have evolved over time provides insight into the dynamic nature of cultural and religious development.

Encouraging Critical Thinking Skills

Analyzing and Comparing

Critical Examination: Encouraging students to critically analyze and compare myths and religious stories from different cultures promotes deeper understanding of their meanings and implications.

Identifying Patterns: Comparing narratives helps students identify patterns and variations in how cultures address fundamental questions about existence, morality, and the divine.

Evaluating Sources

Source Analysis: Teaching students to evaluate the reliability and perspective of sources helps them understand the construction of historical and cultural narratives.

Contextual Understanding: Analyzing the context in which myths and religious texts were written helps students appreciate the historical and cultural factors that influenced these narratives.

Ethical and Philosophical Inquiry

Moral Lessons: Exploring the ethical and philosophical lessons embedded in myths and religious stories encourages students to reflect on their own values and beliefs.

Existential Questions: Discussing the existential questions raised by creation myths and religious narratives helps students engage with profound aspects of human experience.

Viewing Myths, Culture, and Religion as Collective Human History

Interconnected Narratives

Unified Human Experience: Understanding myths and religious stories as part of a collective human history highlights how different cultures grapple with similar existential questions and human experiences.

Cultural Exchange: Recognizing the influences and exchanges between cultures helps students see how myths and religious beliefs have shaped and been shaped by interactions among societies.

Shared Human Values

Universal Themes: Identifying universal themes and values (e.g., the struggle between order and chaos, the quest for meaning) across myths and religious traditions emphasizes common aspects of the human condition.

Cultural Appreciation: Appreciating diverse cultural expressions while recognizing shared human concerns fosters a sense of global interconnectedness and mutual respect.

Reflecting on Contemporary Relevance

Modern Implications: Analyzing how ancient myths and religious beliefs continue to influence modern culture, art, and thought helps students understand the enduring relevance of these narratives.

Ethical Reflection: Reflecting on the moral and ethical teachings of myths and religions in contemporary contexts encourages students to think critically about their own beliefs and actions.

Implementing a Humane Homeschool Approach

Inclusive Curriculum

Diverse Materials: Incorporate texts, stories, and resources from a variety of cultural and religious perspectives to provide a well rounded view of human history and thought.

Balanced Representation: Ensure that diverse perspectives are represented fairly and accurately, avoiding stereotypes and biases.

Interactive Learning

Discussion and Debate: Facilitate discussions and debates on myths and religious stories to encourage students to articulate their understanding and engage with different viewpoints.

Creative Projects: Use creative projects (e.g., storytelling, art, drama) to help students express and explore their understanding of myths and cultural narratives.

Critical Reflection

Reflective Practice: Encourage students to reflect on their learning and consider how different myths and religious beliefs shape their understanding of the world.

Ongoing Inquiry: Promote a culture of inquiry and curiosity, encouraging students to ask questions and seek deeper understanding of the narratives and traditions they study.

By integrating diverse perspectives and fostering critical thinking, a humane homeschool approach helps students see myths, culture, and religion as interconnected threads in the rich tapestry of collective human history. This approach not only enhances their understanding of different cultural and religious traditions but also promotes empathy, respect, and a deeper appreciation of the shared human experience.

Understanding "Child Find"

What is "Child Find"?

Legal Obligation: "Child Find" is a legal requirement under the Individuals with Disabilities Education Act (IDEA). It mandates that public schools actively seek out, identify, and evaluate children who may have disabilities and are in need of special education services.

Purpose: The goal of "Child Find" is to ensure that all eligible children with disabilities are identified and provided with appropriate educational services.

Parent's Role in Child Find

Initiating the Process: While schools have an obligation to identify children who may need special education services, parents play a crucial role in this process. If parents suspect their child has a learning difficulty or disability, they should take proactive steps to seek evaluation and support.

Observation and Documentation: Parents should observe their child's learning and developmental progress and document any concerns. This information can be useful when seeking evaluations and services.

Seeking Support through Health Insurance

Private Evaluations

Health Insurance: Parents can seek evaluations through their health insurance provider to assess learning difficulties or disabilities. These evaluations are often conducted by licensed professionals such as psychologists, neuropsychologists, or developmental pediatricians.

Insurance Coverage: Check with your health insurance provider to understand what types of evaluations are covered, including any necessary referrals or preauthorization requirements.

Benefits of Private Evaluations

Comprehensive Assessment: Private evaluations can provide a detailed assessment of a child's cognitive, emotional, and developmental needs.

Specialized Expertise: Private evaluators may offer specialized expertise in particular areas of learning difficulties or disabilities.

Seeking Support through the Local School District

Requesting Evaluation

Formal Request: Parents can formally request an evaluation from their local school district if they suspect their child has a disability. This request should be made in writing and submitted to the school's special education coordinator or the designated official.

Evaluation Process: Once a request is made, the school district is required to evaluate the child within a specific timeframe to determine if the child has a disability and if they are eligible for special education services.

Types of Support

Individualized Education Program (IEP): If a child is found eligible for special education services, the school will develop an Individualized Education Program (IEP) outlining the specific supports and services the child will receive.

504 Plan: For children who do not qualify for special education but still need accommodations, the school may create a 504 Plan under Section 504 of the Rehabilitation Act.

Navigating the Process

Collaboration with Schools

Engage with Educators: Work closely with teachers, school counselors, and special education staff to address your child's needs and understand the resources available within the school.

FollowUp: Stay engaged in the evaluation process and follow up to ensure that any recommended services or accommodations are implemented effectively.

Advocacy and Resources

Educational Advocacy: Consider seeking the assistance of educational advocates or consultants who specialize in special education to navigate the process and ensure that your child's rights are upheld.

Parent Resources: Utilize resources such as parent support groups, special education organizations, and online communities to gain additional support and information.

In summary, while LEAs have a legal obligation to identify and evaluate children with potential disabilities through "Child Find," parents also have a critical role in initiating the process if they suspect their child may have a learning difficulty or disability. Parents can seek evaluations through their health insurance provider or request support from their local school district. Being proactive in seeking evaluations, collaborating with educational professionals, and utilizing available resources ensures that children receive the necessary support to thrive academically and developmentally.

Understanding Neurodiversity and Biodiversity

Neurodiversity

Definition: Neurodiversity refers to the concept that neurological variations, such as autism, ADHD, dyslexia, and other cognitive differences, are part of the natural spectrum of human diversity rather than disorders to be fixed. It emphasizes valuing and accommodating different ways of thinking and processing information.

Heritability: Many neurodivergent traits are highly heritable, meaning they can run in families. Genetic predisposition can influence the likelihood of neurodivergent traits appearing in offspring.

Biodiversity

Definition: Biodiversity refers to the variety of life forms on Earth, including plants, animals, fungi, and microorganisms. It is essential for ecosystem stability and resilience, providing a rich tapestry of life that supports the health and functionality of natural systems.

Interconnectedness: Just as biodiversity contributes to the robustness of ecosystems, neurodiversity contributes to the richness and adaptability of human communities by bringing diverse perspectives and problem solving approaches.

Heritability and Suitability of Neurodivergent Parents as Educators

Heritability of Neurodivergent Traits

Genetic Factors: Neurodivergent traits are often hereditary, meaning that neurodivergent parents are more likely to have neurodivergent children. This genetic link can create a shared understanding and experience between parents and children.

Empathy and Insight: Neurodivergent parents may have a unique insight into their child's experiences and challenges, fostering a deeper empathy and tailored support that aligns with their child's cognitive and emotional needs.

Benefits of Neurodivergent Parents as Educators

Personal Experience: Neurodivergent parents can draw from their own experiences and coping strategies to provide relevant and effective guidance. Their understanding of neurodivergent learning styles can lead to more effective teaching methods and accommodations.

Customized Support: They can create a learning environment that aligns with their child's needs, offering personalized instruction and support that might be difficult to find in traditional educational settings.

A Brief History of Education

Ancient Civilizations

Sumerians (circa 3000–2000 BCE): The Sumerians, one of the earliest known civilizations, developed the first known writing system, cuneiform, which was used for recording transactions, laws, and literature. Education was primarily reserved for the elite and focused on training scribes and administrators in reading, writing, and arithmetic.

Ancient Greeks (circa 500–300 BCE): The Greeks are credited with laying the groundwork for Western education. They introduced formal schooling for boys, emphasizing a well rounded education that included philosophy, rhetoric, mathematics, and physical education. Notable figures like Socrates, Plato, and Aristotle contributed to educational theory and practice. Plato founded the Academy, one of the first institutions of higher learning.

Romans (circa 500 BCE–500 CE): Roman education was heavily influenced by Greek practices. It focused on preparing young men for public life and included subjects like rhetoric, law, and literature. The Romans also developed the concept of "ludus" (elementary education) and "paedagogium" (higher education), with education becoming more structured and formalized.

Middle Ages and Renaissance

Medieval Period (circa 500–1500 CE): Education during the Middle Ages was largely controlled by the Church. Monasteries and cathedral schools became centers of learning, where scholars studied religious texts, classical works, and emerging sciences. The education was predominantly in Latin, and there was a strong focus on theological studies.

Renaissance (14th–17th Century): The Renaissance sparked a revival of interest in classical learning and humanism. This period saw the emergence of printing technology, which made books more accessible. Educational content expanded to include a broader range of subjects, including art, science, and exploration.

Early Modern Period and Industrial Revolution

Hornbooks (16th–17th Century): In England, hornbooks were used as educational tools for young children. They consisted of a wooden paddle with a sheet of paper covered in a thin layer of horn. This early educational tool helped children learn the alphabet and basic reading skills. Hornbooks can be seen as precursors to modern educational tablets.

McGuffey Readers (19th Century): The McGuffey Readers, a series of textbooks published in the 19th century, were widely used in American schools. They focused on phonics based reading instruction and moral lessons. The readers played a significant role in standardizing literacy education in the United States.

Phonics Flash Cards and Professor Zachos: Phonics flash cards became popular tools for teaching reading through phonics, emphasizing the relationship between letters and sounds. Professor John Zachos' phonics methods contributed to structured literacy approaches, which are still influential in teaching reading today.

The Shift to Public School Systems

Industrial Revolution (18th–19th Century): Upton Sinclair, in his works, documented the shift from traditional homeschooling and community education to a more formalized public school system. The industrial revolution brought about significant changes, including urbanization and the need for a standardized education system to prepare children for industrial work. This led to the development of public schools that operated more like businesses, with a focus on efficiency and uniformity.

Modern Education

Contemporary Era: Today, education continues to evolve, with a focus on integrating technology, addressing diverse learning needs, and adapting to global changes. The English language, with its 26 letters and 44 phonemes, reflects the complexities of language learning. Educational tools and methods have advanced from hornbooks to digital tablets, and the focus on phonics and structured literacy remains crucial in teaching reading effectively.

From the Sumerians' early writing systems to the modern public education system, the history of education reveals a continuous evolution shaped by cultural, technological, and societal changes. Each era has contributed to the development of educational practices and tools, reflecting the needs and values of its time. Understanding this history helps us appreciate the progress made and the ongoing efforts to improve education for future generations.

Historical Context and the Evolution of Homeschooling

John Holt and Historical School Issues

John Holt, a prominent advocate for homeschooling, observed that issues within the educational system are not new. He argued that educational challenges have existed long before the mid20th century and that homeschooling has always been a viable alternative for families seeking a different approach. Holt's perspective highlights that systemic problems in schooling—such as lack of personalization, inadequate resources, and rigid structures—have persisted throughout history.

Historical Homeschooling and Segregation

Before the widespread adoption of public schooling, many families, including those in the segregated South, relied on homeschooling as a practical solution. During the late 19th and early 20th centuries, African American families often turned to homeschooling as a means of circumventing discriminatory practices in the public school system. Benjamin Griffith Brawley, an educator and author documented "The Vale of Tears" (1890–1910), how many African American families, facing educational inequities and segregation, returned or started homeschooling to provide a more equitable and supportive learning environment for their children.

Founding Fathers and Early American Education

Homeschooling has historical roots in early American education. Many of the Founding Fathers of the United States were homeschooled or received their early education at home. This approach allowed for a tailored education that could accommodate their individual needs and interests. Notable figures such as Thomas Jefferson, Benjamin Franklin, and John Adams experienced forms of homeschooling that laid the foundation for their future contributions to American society.

Modern Examples of Homeschooling Success

In contemporary times, homeschooling continues to be associated with notable achievements. Many Olympic athletes, entrepreneurs, and innovators have benefited from homeschooling. For instance:

Olympic Athletes: Several Olympic athletes have been homeschooled to accommodate their rigorous training schedules and individualized needs. Homeschooling provided them with the flexibility to balance their academic and athletic pursuits effectively.

Entrepreneurs and Innovators: Numerous successful entrepreneurs and tech innovators were homeschooled, benefiting from a customized learning environment that fostered creativity and independence. Many notable figures have publicly acknowledged the advantages of homeschooling in their early education. Lots of them also homeschool their own children today.

Neurodivergent Individuals and Homeschooling

Homeschooling is often a valuable option for neurodivergent individuals, providing an adaptable learning environment that can address their unique needs. The flexibility of homeschooling allows for personalized instruction, which can be particularly beneficial for students with conditions such as ADHD, dyslexia, or autism. The success of neurodivergent individuals in various fields underscores the effectiveness of a tailored educational approach.

Homeschooling has a rich historical context that reflects its role as a flexible and adaptive educational approach. From the challenges faced by African American families in the segregated South to the achievements of notable historical figures and modern success stories, homeschooling has proven to be a viable and effective alternative. John Holt's observations and historical examples demonstrate that homeschooling has always been a part of the educational landscape, offering solutions and opportunities that continue to benefit diverse learners today.

Homeschooling as an Effective Educational Approach

Homeschooling Benefits

Personalized Learning: Homeschooling allows for highly individualized instruction tailored to the child's learning style, pace, and interests. This is particularly advantageous for neurodivergent students who may require specialized approaches.

Flexibility: Homeschooling offers flexibility in curriculum design and scheduling, accommodating the specific needs and preferences of both the child and the parent. This can be especially beneficial when addressing sensory sensitivities, attention challenges, or unique learning preferences.

Addressing Limitations of Public and Private Schools

Underfunded Public Schools: Public schools, particularly those that are underfunded, may struggle to provide adequate support for neurodivergent students due to limited resources and a one size fits all approach. Homeschooling can offer more targeted interventions and personalized support.

Inefficient Private Schools: Some private schools may not be equipped to handle the diverse needs of neurodivergent students, especially if they lack specialized staff or resources. Homeschooling allows parents to bypass these limitations and provide a more customized educational experience.

Implementing a Humane Homeschool Approach

Creating a Supportive Environment

Understanding and Acceptance: Establish an environment that values neurodiversity and fosters acceptance. Emphasize strengths and celebrate achievements to build confidence and motivation.

Tailored Instruction: Use teaching methods and materials that align with the child's learning style, such as visual aids, handson activities, or technology tools. Adapt the curriculum to meet the child's specific needs and interests.

Encouraging Growth and Resilience

StrengthBased Approach: Focus on the child's strengths and interests, incorporating them into the learning process to enhance engagement and success.

Promoting SelfAdvocacy: Teach self advocacy skills, allowing the child to understand and articulate their needs and preferences. This fosters independence and resilience.

Neurodiversity and biodiversity share a fundamental principle: diversity contributes to the overall richness and adaptability of systems, whether biological or cognitive. Neurodivergent traits are highly heritable, and neurodivergent parents often possess valuable insights and empathy that can enhance their effectiveness as educators for their neurodivergent children. Homeschooling offers a unique opportunity to provide customized, supportive education that may be more challenging to achieve in underfunded or inefficient public and private school settings. By leveraging their personal experiences and understanding, neurodivergent parents can create a humane and effective homeschooling environment that meets their child's specific needs and fosters a supportive learning journey.

Homeschooling and Permissive Parenting

Permissive Parenting

Definition: Permissive parenting is characterized by a high level of warmth and affection but with minimal rules, structure, or boundaries. This approach may lead to a lack of consistency and discipline, which can impact a child's behavior and academic progress.

Homeschooling Challenges: Homeschooling requires a balance of nurturing support with structure and accountability. Permissive parenting may not provide the necessary framework for effective teaching and learning, leading to potential academic and behavioral issues.

Importance of Structure

Consistency and Boundaries: Effective homeschooling involves setting clear expectations, maintaining consistent routines, and enforcing boundaries. This structure is crucial for creating a productive learning environment and supporting a child's educational and developmental needs.

Understanding and Implementing Mandated Reporting

Mandated Reporting

Legal Obligation: As educators, including homeschooling parents, are considered mandated reporters under the law. This means they are legally required to report suspected cases of child abuse or neglect.

Training: Parents should seek professional development on mandated reporting to understand their responsibilities, recognize signs of abuse or neglect, and know the proper procedures for reporting.

Recognizing Signs of Abuse and Neglect

Physical Abuse: Unexplained injuries, bruises, burns, or fractures.

Emotional Abuse: Extreme behavioral changes, withdrawal, or overly compliant behavior.

Neglect: Poor hygiene, malnutrition, untreated medical issues, or unsafe living conditions.

Sexual Abuse: Difficulty walking or sitting, inappropriate sexual behavior, or fearfulness around certain individuals.

Reporting Abuse

Contact Local Authorities: Report suspected abuse or neglect to local child protective services (CPS) or law enforcement. Provide detailed information and any evidence or observations that led to the suspicion.

Confidentiality: Reports can often be made anonymously to protect the identity of the reporter. Local agencies have procedures in place to maintain confidentiality and prevent retaliation.

Maintaining Anonymity

Anonymous Reporting: Use anonymous reporting options provided by local authorities or child protection agencies. Many jurisdictions offer confidential hotlines or online reporting forms.

Protection from Retaliation: Agencies and organizations have protocols to protect the identities of reporters to prevent retaliation. It is important to follow up with authorities to ensure that appropriate action is being taken.

Professional Development for Homeschooling Parents

Training and Resources

Workshops and Courses: Enroll in workshops, online courses, or local training programs on child protection and mandated reporting. These resources provide valuable knowledge and skills for recognizing and addressing abuse and neglect.

Local Agencies: Contact local child protection agencies or educational organizations for guidance and resources on mandated reporting and child safety.

Ongoing Learning

Stay Informed: Keep updated on changes in child protection laws, reporting procedures, and best practices for ensuring child safety. Engage in continuous learning to enhance your understanding and preparedness.

Homeschooling requires a structured approach to be effective, and permissive parenting may not provide the necessary boundaries and consistency. As homeschooling parents, it is crucial to understand the legal responsibilities related to mandated reporting of child abuse and neglect. Seeking professional development on these topics helps ensure that parents are equipped to recognize and report signs of abuse, maintain anonymity to protect themselves from retaliation, and contribute to the safety and wellbeing of their child and others. Ensuring that all educators, including homeschooling parents, are knowledgeable about their responsibilities and equipped with the necessary skills is essential for creating a safe and supportive learning environment.

Understanding Autonomy and Independence

Autonomy

Definition: Autonomy refers to the ability to make independent choices and decisions. It involves giving children the freedom to take charge of their learning and personal development while still providing guidance and support.

AgeAppropriate Application: Start by offering small choices and responsibilities that match the child's developmental stage. As they grow older, gradually increase the complexity of decisions they can make.

Independence

Definition: Independence is the ability to work and learn on one's own. It involves self reliance, problem solving, and taking initiative.

AgeAppropriate Application: Encourage age appropriate tasks that build self sufficiency, such as managing their own schedule, completing assignments with minimal supervision, or engaging in independent projects.

Implementing Mentorship

Role of Mentorship

Definition: Mentorship involves guiding and supporting a child's growth and development through advice, encouragement, and modeling. It is a relationship where the mentor helps the mentee navigate challenges and achieve goals.

AgeAppropriate Application: Provide mentorship by offering guidance, sharing experiences, and helping the child set and achieve goals. Use open dialogue to understand their interests and challenges and provide support tailored to their needs.

Strategies for Effective Mentorship

Active Listening: Practice active listening to understand the child's perspective and needs. This helps build trust and shows respect for their thoughts and feelings.

Goal Setting: Collaborate with the child to set realistic and achievable goals. Support them in creating a plan and celebrate their progress and achievements.

Fostering a Healthy Interdependent Relationship

Building a Strong Bond

Shared Activities: Engage in activities that promote bonding, such as shared projects, discussions, and problem solving tasks. This strengthens the relationship and provides opportunities for meaningful interactions.

Respect and Trust: Show respect for the child's opinions and decisions. Trust them to take on responsibilities and make choices, reinforcing their confidence and sense of competence.

Maintaining Healthy Boundaries

Clear Expectations: Set clear expectations and boundaries regarding roles and responsibilities. Ensure that the child understands their role in the homeschooling environment and respects the parent's role as both educator and caregiver.

Balance of Power: Avoid letting ego or control dominate the relationship. Recognize that while parents guide and support, children should also have a voice in their learning process.

Modeling an Affirming Relationship

Positive Communication

Encouragement: Acknowledge effort and progress. Offer constructive feedback and focus on strengths rather than shortcomings.

Open Dialogue: Maintain open lines of communication, allowing the child to express their thoughts, feelings, and concerns. Engage in regular conversations about their learning experiences and personal growth.

Empathy and Understanding

Emotional Support: Provide emotional support and understanding, especially when the child faces challenges or setbacks. Validate their feelings and offer reassurance and guidance.

Respectful Interaction: Treat the child with respect and kindness, modeling healthy interactions and relationships. Demonstrate empathy and understanding in all communications.

Encouraging Healthy Communication

Active Engagement

Interactive Learning: Engage in interactive learning experiences that encourage dialogue and feedback. Foster an environment where questions are welcomed and curiosity is encouraged.

ProblemSolving Together: Work through problems and challenges together, allowing the child to contribute their ideas and solutions. This promotes critical thinking and collaborative learning.

Conflict Resolution

Constructive Discussion: Approach conflicts or disagreements with a constructive mindset. Use problem solving techniques and encourage open discussion to find solutions.

Modeling Behavior: Model respectful and effective communication strategies. Demonstrate how to handle disagreements calmly and professionally.

In a homeschool setting, integrating autonomy, independence, and mentorship in an age appropriate manner helps foster a healthy, interdependent relationship between parents and children. By offering choices and responsibilities, providing guidance and support, and maintaining clear boundaries, parents can build a strong bond with their children while avoiding issues of control and ego. Modeling an affirming relationship through positive communication, empathy, and respectful interaction further strengthens the connection and ensures healthy, effective communication. This approach not only supports the child's growth and development but also enhances the overall homeschooling experience.

Age Appropriate Conversations

Addressing important topics such as stress, anxiety, peer pressure, grooming, self defense, perfectionism, imposter syndrome, self advocacy, and bullying requires thoughtful, age appropriate conversations. Parents play a crucial role in discussing these issues with their children and modeling inclusive behavior.

Early Childhood (Ages 37)

Stress and Anxiety: Use simple language to talk about feelings. Introduce concepts of being "worried" or "scared" and offer reassurance. Encourage expression through drawing or storytelling.

Peer Pressure: Teach basic social skills, such as sharing and taking turns. Emphasize the importance of choosing friends who are kind and supportive.

SelfDefense: Focus on basic safety rules, like staying close to trusted adults and understanding the concept of "safe" and "unsafe" touches.

Grooming: Introduce the idea of personal hygiene through fun routines, such as brushing teeth and washing hands.

Inclusion: Model inclusive behavior by playing cooperatively and including others in games. Discuss the importance of kindness and making everyone feel welcome.

Middle Childhood (Ages 812)

Stress and Anxiety: Discuss how to recognize and manage stress through relaxation techniques, such as deep breathing or mindfulness exercises. Encourage open dialogue about their feelings.

Peer Pressure: Explain the concept of peer pressure and discuss strategies for making decisions that are right for them, even if it's not popular. Roleplay scenarios to practice assertiveness.

SelfDefense: Teach more specific self defense strategies, including how to set boundaries and speak up if they feel uncomfortable. Discuss the importance of telling a trusted adult.

Perfectionism: Address the idea that making mistakes is part of learning. Encourage a growth mindset and praise effort rather than just outcomes.

Imposter Syndrome: Help them understand that everyone has strengths and weaknesses. Normalize feelings of self doubt and emphasize that their worth is not tied to their achievements.

SelfAdvocacy: Encourage them to express their needs and opinions clearly and respectfully. Teach them how to ask for help when needed.

Bullying and Exclusion: Explain what bullying is and how to seek help. Roleplay responses to bullying and discuss how to support friends who might be excluded.

Inclusion: Promote inclusivity by celebrating diversity and ensuring they understand the value of including everyone in activities and conversations.

Adolescence (Ages 1318)

Stress and Anxiety: Discuss more complex stressors, such as academic pressures and social dynamics. Explore healthy coping strategies, such as exercise, hobbies, and seeking professional help if needed.

Peer Pressure: Discuss real life scenarios related to peer pressure and explore strategies for resisting negative influences. Emphasize the importance of staying true to oneself.

SelfDefense: Teach about personal safety in various situations, including online safety. Discuss the importance of trust and setting boundaries in relationships.

Perfectionism: Address the impact of perfectionism on mental health and productivity. Encourage a balanced approach to goals and achievements.

Imposter Syndrome: Discuss how to manage feelings of inadequacy and celebrate their accomplishments. Encourage them to seek mentorship and peer support.

SelfAdvocacy: Support them in developing strong self advocacy skills, such as negotiating, problem solving, and asserting their needs effectively.

Bullying and Exclusion: Discuss strategies for dealing with bullying and exclusion, including how to report issues and seek support. Encourage them to be allies and stand up against bullying.

Inclusion: Foster an understanding of social justice and the importance of inclusivity. Discuss ways to promote inclusion in their communities and schools.

Fostering and Modeling Inclusion

Modeling Inclusive Behavior

Demonstrate Respect: Show respect and kindness to others in your daily interactions. Treat everyone with dignity, regardless of differences.

Celebrate Diversity: Engage in activities that celebrate various cultures, traditions, and perspectives. Highlight the value of diversity in your discussions and experiences.

Creating an Inclusive Environment

Encourage Open Dialogue: Foster an environment where everyone feels safe to express their thoughts and feelings. Address any issues of exclusion or discrimination promptly and sensitively.

Supportive Community: Build a supportive community around your child that values inclusivity and respect. Encourage participation in activities that promote understanding and empathy.

Educational Resources

Books and Media: Use age appropriate books, movies, and educational materials that highlight themes of inclusion and diversity. Discuss the lessons and values depicted in these resources.

Community Involvement: Involve your child in community events and programs that focus on inclusivity and social justice. Provide opportunities for them to learn about and engage with diverse groups.

Addressing topics such as stress, anxiety, peer pressure, grooming, self defense, perfectionism, imposter syndrome, self advocacy, and bullying requires age appropriate discussions and strategies. Parents should integrate these conversations into their homeschooling approach, modeling inclusive behavior and fostering a supportive environment. By addressing these issues thoughtfully and respectfully, parents can help their children navigate challenges, build resilience, and develop strong interpersonal skills.

Transitioning back to Traditional School before High School

Evaluating the Current Status

Assess Academic Progress: Review your child's academic records, including completed coursework, grades, and standardized test results. Gather documentation such as transcripts, report cards, and any records of achievements or extracurricular activities.

Understand School Requirements: Research the specific requirements and admission processes for public or private schools in your area. Different schools may have varying criteria for grade placement and curriculum equivalency.

Re Enrolling in Public or Private School

Contact Local Schools: Reach out to local public or private schools to inquire about their enrollment procedures. Schedule meetings with school administrators or counselors to discuss your child's academic background and transition needs.

Submit Documentation: Provide the necessary documentation to the school, including academic records, proof of residency, and any required application forms.

Placement Testing: Some schools may require placement tests to determine the appropriate grade level or coursework for your child. Prepare your child for these assessments if needed.

Addressing Social and Emotional Adjustments

Support Transition: Prepare your child for the transition by discussing what to expect in their new school environment. Encourage open communication about any concerns or anxieties they may have.

Social Integration: Facilitate opportunities for your child to meet peers and participate in school activities to ease social integration.

Transitioning During High School

Reentering High School

Research Options: Investigate public and private high schools in your area and their specific enrollment requirements. Some schools may have specialized programs or support for students transitioning from homeschooling.

Prepare Documentation: Similar to transitioning before high school, gather and submit necessary documentation, including academic records and application forms. Be prepared for placement testing or interviews as required.

Alternative Education Options

Dual Enrollment: Explore dual enrollment options where your child can take college level courses at a local community college or online while still in high school. This can provide advanced academic opportunities and facilitate a smoother transition to higher education.

GED and High School Equivalency Exams: If reentering high school is not feasible or desirable, consider alternative paths such as obtaining a General Educational Development (GED) certificate. Other high school equivalency exams include the HiSET and TASC. Research the requirements and testing locations for these exams.

CLEP Tests: The CollegeLevel Examination Program (CLEP) offers exams that can earn college credit for knowledge acquired outside of a traditional classroom setting. This option can accelerate academic progress and provide flexibility.

AP Tests: Advanced Placement (AP) tests allow high school students to earn college credit by demonstrating proficiency in specific subject areas. Investigate available AP courses and exams at local high schools or online.

Standardized Tests: Prepare for standardized tests such as the PSAT, SAT, or ACT, which are commonly used for college admissions and can also provide valuable academic benchmarks.

Taking a Break: If your child needs additional time to adjust or explore their interests, consider taking a break from formal education. They can use this time to work, gain life experiences, or explore vocational training.

Using FAFSA and College Placement Exams

FAFSA and College Placement: For students considering higher education later, they can use the Free Application for Federal Student Aid (FAFSA) once they turn 2 This allows them to apply for financial aid based on their own income and educational needs. They can also take college placement exams to determine the appropriate level of college courses.

Transitioning from homeschooling to public or private school before high school involves evaluating academic progress, contacting local schools, and preparing for placement tests. During high school, reentry can be more complex, but there are alternative education options such as dual enrollment, GED, HiSET, TASC, CLEP tests, AP tests, standardized tests, and taking a break. For students considering higher education later, they can use FAFSA for financial aid and take college placement exams. Each option has its own requirements and benefits, and it's important to explore these based on your child's individual needs and goals.

Transcripts

Creating Transcripts

Record Keeping: Parents are responsible for maintaining accurate and comprehensive academic records throughout the high school years. This includes recording grades, course titles, credits earned, and any standardized test scores.

Transcript Generation: At the end of each academic year or upon graduation, parents should compile these records into a formal transcript. This document should list all courses completed, grades received, and any extracurricular activities or achievements.

Transcript Requirements

Standard Format: Ensure the transcript follows a standard format, including the student's name, date of birth, graduation date, and a detailed listing of coursework and grades. Some homeschool support organizations offer transcript templates or services.

Verification: If the student applies to colleges or other institutions, the transcript may need to be verified or notarized to confirm its authenticity.

Vaccination Records

Maintaining Records

Health Documentation: Keep detailed records of your child's vaccinations and medical history. This is important for compliance with public health requirements and for any future educational or employment needs.

Access to Records: Ensure that vaccination records are readily accessible and can be provided upon request for school enrollment, college applications, or other official purposes.

State Requirements

Check State Regulations: Different states have varying requirements regarding vaccination records for homeschooled students. Ensure compliance with your state's regulations and keep uptodate records.

Identification

Obtaining Identification

Driver's License or Permit: If your child is of driving age, they will need to obtain a driver's license or learner's permit. This process typically involves passing written and practical tests.

State ID: If a driver's license is not desired or feasible, obtain a state identification card. This card serves as an official form of identification and is useful for various purposes.

Importance of Identification

Access to Services: A valid ID is necessary for activities such as applying for jobs, opening bank accounts, and accessing certain services.

Verification: Identification may be required for official documentation and processes, such as college applications or government services.

Issuing a Diploma

Creating a Diploma

Design and Content: Parents are responsible for designing and issuing a high school diploma. The diploma should include the student's name, graduation date, and the name of the homeschooling entity (e.g., a family name or educational organization).

Diploma Format: Ensure that the diploma follows a professional format and includes necessary details, such as the signature of the parent or guardian who is acting as the school administrator.

Recognition and Use

Acceptance: Many colleges, universities, and employers accept diplomas issued by homeschooling families, but it's a good idea to check with specific institutions to ensure they recognize the diploma.

Transcript and Diploma: Provide both the diploma and transcript as part of the student's application process for higher education or employment.

When homeschooling through high school, parents are fully responsible for several key administrative tasks:

Transcripts: Maintaining and generating detailed academic records.

Vaccination Records: Keeping uptodate health documentation.

Identification: Obtaining necessary forms of identification, such as a driver's license or state ID.

Diploma: Issuing a high school diploma, including designing and verifying its contents.

By handling these responsibilities, parents ensure that their homeschooled student is well prepared for postsecondary education, employment, and other life transitions. It's important to stay organized and informed about state requirements and institutional expectations to support the student's future opportunities effectively.

Understanding State Specific Homeschool Laws

Registration and Notification

State Requirements: Most states require parents to notify or register their intent to homeschool with the local school district or state education department. This may involve submitting a letter of intent, an affidavit, or completing specific forms.

Deadlines: Be aware of deadlines for notifying the appropriate authorities at the beginning of each school year or upon starting homeschooling.

Curriculum and Instruction

Curriculum Requirements: Some states have specific requirements regarding the subjects and instructional hours that must be covered. Familiarize yourself with these requirements to ensure compliance.

Instructional Methods: States may have guidelines on instructional methods and materials, including whether standardized tests or specific educational standards must be met.

Record Keeping

Academic Records: Maintain detailed records of your child's educational progress, including lesson plans, grades, attendance, and assessments. This documentation may be required for periodic evaluations or in case of disputes.

Transcripts: For high school students, keep a transcript of courses, grades, and credits earned, which is essential for college applications and other postsecondary plans.

Health and Safety Regulations

Vaccination Records

Health Documentation: Some states require proof of vaccinations or exemptions if homeschooling. Keep accurate records of your child's immunizations and be aware of any state specific requirements.

Health and Safety Standards

Safety Regulations: Ensure that your homeschooling environment meets basic health and safety standards. This includes having a safe learning space and addressing any potential hazards.

Special Education and Accommodations

Identification and Services

Child Find: If you suspect your child has special education needs, you are responsible for identifying and seeking support, either through public school evaluations or private assessments.

IEPs and 504 Plans: If your child has an Individualized Education Plan (IEP) or a 504 Plan from a previous school, understand how these accommodations can be implemented in a homeschooling setting.

Assessment and Evaluation

Standardized Testing

Testing Requirements: Some states require homeschooled students to take standardized tests to measure academic progress. Be aware of the testing requirements and schedule assessments as needed.

Alternative Assessments: If standardized testing is not required, consider alternative methods of assessment, such as portfolios, projects, or other evaluations.

Annual Evaluations

Performance Reviews: Certain states mandate annual evaluations of homeschooled students' progress. These evaluations might include assessments by certified teachers, standardized tests, or portfolio reviews.

Legal Protections and Rights

Educational Rights

Homeschooling Laws: Stay informed about state and federal homeschooling laws to ensure that you are exercising your rights and fulfilling your obligations.

Legal Resources: Join homeschooling associations or legal defense organizations for support and updates on changes in homeschooling laws.

Child Welfare and Reporting

Mandatory Reporting: Understand your responsibilities as a mandated reporter. Familiarize yourself with signs of abuse and neglect and know how to report any concerns to the appropriate authorities.

Legal Protections: Ensure that you are aware of legal protections for homeschooling families and how to address any issues related to your child's welfare or educational rights.

Transitioning Out of Homeschooling

Re Enrollment Procedures

Local School District: If you decide to transition back to public or private school, follow the procedures for re enrollment, including providing academic records, vaccination records, and any other required documentation.

Equivalency Exams: If transitioning during high school, consider options such as obtaining a GED or other high school equivalency tests if appropriate.

When homeschooling from K12, parents need to stay updated with various legal requirements, including:

Registration and Notification: Notify local authorities of your intent to homeschool and adhere to any registration requirements.

Curriculum and Instruction: Follow state guidelines for curriculum, instructional hours, and educational standards.

Record Keeping: Maintain accurate records of academic progress and transcripts.

Health and Safety: Comply with health documentation requirements and ensure a safe learning environment.

Special Education: Seek necessary evaluations and accommodations for students with special needs.

Assessment and Evaluation: Adhere to standardized testing and evaluation requirements.

Legal Protections: Stay informed about your educational rights and responsibilities, including mandatory reporting.

Transitioning: Follow procedures for re enrolling in public or private schools if necessary.

By understanding and adhering to these legal requirements, parents can effectively manage their homeschooling journey and ensure compliance with state and federal regulations.

Understanding the 14th Amendment

Due Process Clause

Protection of Rights: The 14th Amendment's Due Process Clause states that no state shall deprive any person of life, liberty, or property without due process of law. This clause has been interpreted to protect various individual rights, including parental rights.

Parental Rights: Courts have recognized that the Due Process Clause includes a fundamental right for parents to make decisions regarding the care, custody, and upbringing of their children. This includes the right to direct their child's education and upbringing.

Equal Protection Clause

NonDiscrimination: The Equal Protection Clause of the 14th Amendment mandates that no state shall deny any person within its jurisdiction the equal protection of the laws. This ensures that all individuals, including parents, are treated equally and fairly under the law.

Parental Rights Under the 14th Amendment

Education Decisions

Homeschooling: The right to direct a child's education is protected under the 14th Amendment. This includes the right to choose homeschooling and to determine the educational content and methods used.

Curriculum Choice: Parents have the authority to select the curriculum and educational materials they deem appropriate for their children, as long as they comply with state education laws and standards.

Access to Information

Control Over Information: The 14th Amendment protects parental rights to make decisions about the information their child has access to, including educational content, media exposure, and other information that may impact their child's development and beliefs.

Privacy: Parents have the right to shield their children from information or content they believe is inappropriate or harmful, within the bounds of the law. This includes making choices about their child's exposure to various topics and ensuring that educational materials align with their family values and beliefs.

Legal Precedents and Parental Rights

Landmark Cases

Pierce v. Society of Sisters (1925): The Supreme Court ruled that parents have the right to choose private or religious schooling for their children rather than attending public schools. This case affirmed the fundamental right of parents to direct their children's education.

Troxel v. Granville (2000): The Supreme Court upheld the right of parents to make decisions concerning the care and upbringing of their children, reinforcing the concept that parental rights are fundamental and protected under the Due Process Clause of the 14th Amendment.

Limitations and Responsibilities

State Regulation

Education Standards: While parents have significant rights under the 14th Amendment, these rights are balanced by state regulations and standards that ensure children receive a basic education. Parents must comply with state laws regarding compulsory education, health and safety requirements, and educational standards.

Child Welfare: Parental rights are also subject to limitations if the welfare of the child is at risk. For example, if a child is being harmed or neglected, state intervention may occur to protect the child's wellbeing.

Balancing Rights and Protections

Rights vs. State Interests: While the 14th Amendment protects parental rights, there are instances where state interests, such as protecting children from harm or ensuring educational standards, may require balancing these rights.

The 14th Amendment of the U.S. Constitution provides a foundation for parental rights in education and childrearing:

Due Process Clause: Protects the right of parents to make decisions about their child's education and upbringing, including the choice to homeschool and select educational content.

Equal Protection Clause: Ensures that parents are treated equally under the law and are not unfairly discriminated against in their role as educators and caregivers.

Legal Precedents: Landmark cases have affirmed the fundamental rights of parents to direct their children's education and access to information.

State Regulations: While parents have significant rights, they must comply with state regulations that ensure educational standards and child welfare.

Understanding these rights and responsibilities helps parents navigate homeschooling and other educational choices while ensuring compliance with legal requirements and protecting their child's wellbeing.

Starting a homeschool program with a focus on humane practices involves prioritizing the student's rights, ensuring a supportive and ethical learning environment, and addressing legal considerations related to child labor if the student chooses to work.

Respect in a Humane Homeschool

Respecting Student Rights

StudentCentered Approach: Design the homeschooling environment to be respectful and responsive to the student's individual needs, interests, and learning styles. This includes creating a supportive atmosphere that values the student's voice and fosters their academic and emotional growth.

Open Communication: Maintain open lines of communication with the student. Encourage them to express their needs, concerns, and preferences regarding their education. Ensure that they feel heard and valued in the homeschooling process.

Ethical Education

Inclusive Curriculum: Develop a curriculum that is inclusive and representative of diverse perspectives. Avoid materials or methods that might perpetuate bias or discrimination.

Holistic Development: Focus on the student's overall development, including social, emotional, and cognitive growth. Provide opportunities for them to engage in activities that promote critical thinking, creativity, and wellbeing.

Preventing Exploitation

Fair Treatment: Ensure that the homeschooling environment is free from any form of exploitation or unfair treatment. The student should not be required to perform tasks or chores that interfere with their education or wellbeing.

WorkLife Balance: Balance academic responsibilities with time for relaxation, hobbies, and social activities. Avoid overburdening the student with excessive academic demands or responsibilities.

Preventing Illegal Child Labor

Understanding Child Labor Laws

Legal Requirements: Familiarize yourself with federal and state child labor laws, which regulate the type of work and the hours minors can legally work. These laws are designed to protect the health and safety of young workers and ensure that their education is not compromised.

Age Restrictions: Be aware of the age specific restrictions on employment. For instance, the Fair Labor Standards Act (FLSA) in the U.S. sets limits on the hours and types of work that minors can engage in, depending on their age.

Educational Priorities

Education First: Ensure that the student's education remains the primary focus. Work opportunities should not interfere with their academic responsibilities or overall wellbeing.

Academic Schedule: Adjust the student's work schedule to accommodate their educational needs. The work should be flexible and not detract from their learning experiences.

Issuing Work Permits

Legal Requirements for Work Permits

Permit Issuance: If the student chooses to work at a young age, you may need to obtain a work permit, depending on state regulations. This process involves obtaining permission from the local school district or another relevant authority.

Documentation: Prepare the necessary documentation, which may include proof of age, school records, and consent forms. Ensure that all paperwork is completed accurately and submitted according to local requirements.

Balancing Work and Education

Work Hours: Adhere to legal limits on the number of hours a minor can work. Ensure that work hours do not exceed the limits set by child labor laws and that they are balanced with the student's educational responsibilities.

Safe Work Environment: Ensure that the work environment is safe and appropriate for the student's age and abilities. The job should provide a positive and enriching experience rather than posing risks to the student's health or safety.

Starting a humane homeschool involves:

Honoring Student Rights: Create a respectful and supportive learning environment that values the student's input and focuses on their holistic development.

Preventing Exploitation: Ensure that the student is not subjected to unfair practices or excessive demands. Maintain a healthy balance between education and other activities.

Understanding Child Labor Laws: Be aware of and comply with child labor laws to protect the student's rights and ensure that work does not interfere with their education.

Issuing Work Permits: If the student chooses to work, follow legal procedures for issuing work permits and ensure that work schedules and conditions comply with regulations.

By adhering to these principles, parents can create a humane and legally compliant homeschooling environment that respects the student's rights and wellbeing while providing opportunities for growth and development.

It's important to foster a collaborative environment in a homeschool setting that aligns the teaching strengths of the parent with the learning strengths of the student involves creating a dynamic and interactive educational atmosphere.

Understanding Strengths and Needs

Identify Teaching Strengths

SelfAssessment: Reflect on your own strengths and expertise as an educator. Consider subjects you're passionate about, your teaching style, and areas where you excel.

Feedback: Seek feedback from the student about what methods work best for them. This can help you understand how your teaching strengths align with their learning preferences.

Recognize Learning Strengths

Learning Preferences: Identify the student's learning preferences and strengths. These might include visual, auditory, kinesthetic, or a combination of styles.

Assessment: Use informal assessments, observations, and conversations to determine how the student learns best and what motivates them.

Creating a Collaborative Learning Environment

Set Shared Goals

Mutual Objectives: Establish clear, shared learning goals with the student. Involve them in setting these goals to ensure they are invested in the process.

Alignment: Align the goals with both your teaching strengths and the student's learning strengths to create a sense of ownership and relevance.

Develop a Flexible Curriculum

Tailored Lessons: Design lessons that leverage your teaching strengths while accommodating the student's learning preferences. For example, if you're skilled in visual presentations and the student is a visual learner, incorporate diagrams and videos.

Adaptation: Be willing to adapt the curriculum based on the student's evolving needs and interests. Flexibility allows for adjustments that enhance learning and engagement.

Encourage Active Participation

Student Involvement: Encourage the student to take an active role in their learning. This can include setting their own learning objectives, selecting projects, and providing input on how they want to learn.

Collaborative Projects: Work on projects together that integrate both your teaching strengths and the student's interests. This promotes teamwork and allows for a deeper exploration of subjects.

Utilizing Effective Communication

Open Dialogue

Regular CheckIns: Have regular discussions with the student about their learning experiences and preferences. This helps you adjust your approach and ensures that the learning environment remains supportive.

Feedback: Provide constructive feedback and encourage the student to share their thoughts on what is working well and what needs improvement.

ProblemSolving Together

Address Challenges: When challenges arise, work together to find solutions. This collaborative approach fosters problem solving skills and helps build a supportive learning environment.

Celebrate Success: Acknowledge and celebrate achievements and progress. Recognizing successes reinforces positive learning experiences and motivates the student.

Integrating Resources and Tools

Utilize Diverse Resources

Learning Materials: Use a variety of learning materials and resources that cater to both your teaching strengths and the student's learning preferences. This can include books, online resources, educational games, and handson activities.

Technology: Incorporate technology as a tool to enhance learning. Choose tools that align with the student's strengths and interests, such as interactive apps or educational software.

Seek External Support

Guest Experts: Invite guest experts or tutors to provide additional perspectives or expertise in areas where you may not be as strong. This can offer the student exposure to different teaching styles and deepen their understanding of subjects.

Community Resources: Engage with community resources such as museums, libraries, and local organizations to provide real world learning experiences that complement your teaching.

Reflecting and Improving

Continuous Improvement

SelfReflection: Regularly reflect on your teaching practices and their effectiveness. Consider how well they align with the student's learning strengths and make adjustments as needed.

Student Feedback: Actively seek and incorporate feedback from the student to continuously improve the learning experience.

Adapt and Evolve

Growth Mindset: Maintain a growth mindset and be open to evolving your teaching methods. As the student's needs and interests change, adapt your approach to ensure continued alignment and effectiveness.

Summary

To foster a collaborative homeschooling environment that supports both the parent's teaching strengths and the student's learning strengths:

Identify and Leverage Strengths: Understand your teaching strengths and the student's learning preferences to tailor your approach.

Set Shared Goals: Establish clear, mutual learning goals and align them with your strengths and the student's needs.

Create a Flexible Curriculum: Develop lessons that accommodate both your strengths and the student's learning style, and be flexible in adapting to their evolving needs.

Encourage Active Participation: Involve the student in their learning process and work together on projects.

Utilize Resources and Tools: Use diverse resources and technology, and seek external support when needed.

Reflect and Improve: Continuously reflect on and adjust your teaching practices based on feedback and changing needs.

By following these steps, parents can create a collaborative and supportive learning environment that enhances the educational experience for both the parent and the student.

Evaluating Curriculum Quality and Effectiveness

Assessing Curriculum Fit

Alignment with Goals: Ensure the curriculum aligns with both the educational goals you've set and the student's learning needs. Evaluate whether it addresses key subjects effectively and engages the student in meaningful ways.

Engagement and Interest: Assess how well the curriculum captures the student's interest and motivates them to learn. Effective curricula often include varied activities and resources that cater to different learning styles.

Measuring Progress

Performance Metrics: Use various assessments (formal and informal) to gauge the student's progress and understanding of the material. Regular quizzes, tests, and assignments can help you measure their grasp of the content.

Feedback and Adjustments: Provide constructive feedback to the student and adjust the curriculum as needed based on their performance and feedback. This helps ensure that the curriculum remains effective and relevant.

Quality of Materials

Resource Evaluation: Evaluate the quality of textbooks, online resources, and other educational materials. Ensure they are accurate, uptodate, and suitable for the student's grade level and learning style.

Resource Variety: Incorporate a variety of resources to keep the learning experience dynamic and engaging. This may include multimedia resources, handson activities, and real world applications.

State Laws on Assessment

Variation in State Regulations

Assessment Requirements: State laws regarding homeschooling assessments vary widely. Some states require standardized testing, while others may have more flexible evaluation methods such as portfolio assessments or teacher evaluations.

Reporting: States may have different requirements for reporting educational progress to local or state education authorities. These can include submitting test scores, evaluation reports, or detailed records of the student's work.

General Guidelines for Assessment

Research State Requirements: Familiarize yourself with your state's specific homeschooling assessment laws and requirements. This information can typically be found on state education department websites or through local homeschooling organizations.

Maintain Records: Keep detailed records of the student's progress and assessments. This includes test scores, completed assignments, and any other relevant documentation.

Regular Evaluations: Conduct regular evaluations to ensure the student is meeting educational milestones and standards. Adjust the curriculum based on these evaluations to address any gaps or areas for improvement.

Responsibility for RecordKeeping and Portfolio Creation

Maintaining Records

Documentation: Maintain accurate and uptodate records of the student's academic progress, including grades, test results, and completed assignments. This documentation is essential for tracking progress and meeting state requirements.

Organized Filing: Keep records organized in a way that makes them easily accessible. This can include digital files or physical folders, depending on your preference and state regulations.

Creating a Portfolio

Portfolio Contents: Develop a portfolio that showcases the student's work over time. This can include samples of completed assignments, projects, written reflections, and assessments.

Regular Updates: Regularly update the portfolio to reflect the student's ongoing progress and achievements. Use it as a tool to review their learning and identify areas for further development.

Maintaining HighQuality Education

Continuous Improvement: Continuously evaluate and improve the curriculum based on the student's needs, progress, and feedback. Be open to adapting teaching methods and materials to enhance the educational experience.

Seek Resources: Utilize available resources, such as educational workshops, online courses, and homeschooling support groups, to stay informed and enhance your teaching practices.

Summary

Parent Responsibility

Evaluate Curriculum: Parents are responsible for assessing the quality and effectiveness of the curriculum to ensure it meets educational goals and engages the student effectively.

State Compliance: Understand and comply with state laws regarding homeschooling assessments, including keeping records and maintaining a high quality education.

RecordKeeping: Keep detailed records and create a portfolio to document the student's progress and achievements.

Continuous Improvement: Regularly evaluate and adjust the curriculum based on the student's progress and feedback to maintain a high standard of education.

By taking these steps, parents can ensure that their homeschooling program provides a high quality education that meets state requirements and supports the student's academic and personal growth.

Setup and Organization

Choose Your Format

Physical Binder: Use a three ring binder with dividers for each section. Consider using plastic sleeves for important documents.

Online Folder: Use a cloud based storage system (e.g., Google Drive, Dropbox) with clearly labeled folders and subfolders.

Create Sections

General Organization: Create main sections for each major category of documents. Each section can have subfolders or tabs for more detailed organization.

Required Documents

Enrollment and Legal Documents

Homeschooling Affidavit: If required by your state, include a copy of your homeschooling affidavit or intent to homeschool.

State Requirements: Document any state specific requirements or forms needed for homeschooling.

Curriculum and Planning

Curriculum Overview: Include a summary of the chosen curriculum and learning objectives for each grade level.

Lesson Plans: Maintain detailed lesson plans or outlines for each subject and grade level.

Scope and Sequence: Provide an overview of the subjects and skills covered throughout the year.

Assessment and Records

Progress Reports: Keep records of student progress, including grades, test scores, and completed assignments.

Annual Assessments: Include results of any required annual assessments or standardized tests.

Attendance Records: Document daily or weekly attendance as required by state regulations.

Student Records

Personal Information: Maintain records of important personal information (e.g., birth certificate, emergency contact information).

Health Records: Include vaccination records, medical history, and any special accommodations or health concerns.

Optional Documents

Educational Materials

Resource List: Keep a list of textbooks, online resources, and supplementary materials used in the curriculum.

Field Trip Records: Document field trips, including dates, locations, and activities.

Student Work and Projects

Portfolio: Maintain a portfolio of student work, including samples of assignments, projects, and creative work.

Achievements: Record any awards, certificates, or recognitions received by the student.

Planning and Reflection

Yearly Goals: Document yearly educational goals and objectives for each student.

Reflections: Include reflections and notes on the effectiveness of the curriculum and teaching methods.

Extracurricular Activities

Activity Records: Track involvement in extracurricular activities, including sports, arts, and community service.

Schedules and Documents: Include schedules, registration forms, and any related correspondence.

Humane Education Documents

Inclusive Practices

Diversity Resources: Include resources and materials that support an inclusive and diverse learning environment.

Neurodiversity Plans: Document any specific accommodations or strategies for supporting neurodivergent students.

Environmental and Ethical Education

Environmental Projects: Keep records of environmental education projects and activities.

Ethics Discussions: Document any discussions or lessons on ethics, social responsibility, and moral reasoning.

Professional Development

Training Records: Include records of any professional development courses or workshops attended by the parent/educator.

Resource List: Maintain a list of books, articles, and resources related to humane education and homeschooling best practices.

Maintenance and Updates

Regular Updates

Document Review: Periodically review and update the contents of the binder or online folder to ensure accuracy and completeness.

Backup: For online folders, ensure regular backups to prevent data loss. For physical binders, consider digitizing important documents.

Access and Security

Physical Security: Store physical documents in a secure and organized manner.

Digital Security: Ensure online folders are password protected and access is restricted to authorized individuals only.

Communication

Sharing Information: If applicable, share relevant documents with local education authorities or support organizations as required.

Feedback: Collect feedback from students and adjust documentation and organization as needed to improve the homeschooling experience.

By following these guidelines, you can create an organized and comprehensive homeschool binder or online document folder that supports a humane and effective educational experience for your children. This system will help you manage records efficiently, stay compliant with legal requirements, and ensure that you are providing the best possible education in a supportive and inclusive environment.

Guideline for Seeking Free Professional Development

Community Resources

Local Libraries and Community Centers

Workshops and Seminars: Check local libraries and community centers for free workshops, seminars, and educational events. These may cover a range of topics including education, parenting, and personal development.

Networking Events: Attend community networking events to connect with local educators and professionals who might offer advice or resources.

Nonprofit Organizations and Advocacy Groups

Educational Nonprofits: Many nonprofit organizations offer free or low cost professional development for parents and educators. Look for local or national organizations focused on education, literacy, or child development.

Support Groups: Join support groups or forums related to homeschooling or education. These can be valuable sources of information and professional development opportunities.

Local School Districts and Education Boards

Parent Workshops: Inquire with your local school district or education board about parent workshops or training sessions. They may offer free resources and training for homeschooling parents.

Cox Campus

Accessing Cox Campus

Website: Visit the Cox Campus website to explore their free professional development resources. They offer courses and webinars designed to support early childhood education.

Registration: Register for an account to access courses and track your progress. Cox Campus provides training on literacy, child development, and effective teaching strategies.

Available Courses

Literacy Training: Look for courses focused on early literacy, phonics, and reading strategies.

Parenting Workshops: Explore workshops on parenting techniques and supporting child development.

Microsoft Learn

Accessing Microsoft Learn

Website: Visit Microsoft Learn to find a wide range of free courses on various topics. While it primarily focuses on technology, it also offers professional development resources that can be beneficial for educators and parents.

Learning Paths: Explore learning paths related to productivity, collaboration, and digital skills that can enhance your ability to support your child's education.

Relevant Content

Digital Tools: Learn about using Microsoft tools (e.g., Word, Excel, OneNote) to organize and plan your homeschooling efforts.

Educational Technology: Discover how to integrate educational technology effectively into your homeschooling routine.

YouTube

Finding Educational Content

Search: Use YouTube to search for free educational videos on a wide range of topics, including homeschooling strategies, teaching methods, and child development.

Channels: Subscribe to reputable educational channels that offer professional development content for parents and educators. Some recommended channels might include CrashCourse and Khan Academy.

Types of Videos

Homeschooling Tips: Find videos that offer practical advice and tips for homeschooling.

Educational Methods: Watch tutorials and lectures on effective teaching methods and educational philosophies.

General Tips

Staying Updated

Email Newsletters: Sign up for newsletters from educational organizations, online learning platforms, and community groups to stay informed about new professional development opportunities.

Engaging with Online Communities

Forums and Groups: Join online forums and social media groups related to homeschooling and education. These platforms often share information about free professional development resources and events.

Setting Goals

Personal Development Plan: Create a plan for your professional development goals. Identify the skills or knowledge you want to acquire and seek out relevant resources and courses.

Leveraging Free Resources

Utilize Free Trials: Some platforms offer free trials or sample courses. Take advantage of these to explore their offerings before committing to any paid resources.

By following these guidelines, you can access a wealth of free professional development opportunities to enhance your homeschooling efforts and support your child's education effectively. These resources will help you stay informed, improve your skills, and provide the best possible learning experience for your children.

Creating a Curriculum

Define Educational Goals

GradeLevel Standards: Review state or national education standards for each grade level to ensure you meet the required learning objectives.

Learning Objectives: Set clear, measurable goals for what students should know and be able to do by the end of each grade.

Choose a Curriculum Framework

Subject Areas: Decide on the subject areas you will cover (e.g., language arts, math, science, social studies).

Educational Philosophy: Align your curriculum with your educational philosophy, whether it's traditional, Montessori, project based learning, etc.

Research and Select Resources

Textbooks and Workbooks: Choose age appropriate textbooks, workbooks, and other educational materials.

Online Resources: Find reputable online resources, including educational websites, videos, and interactive tools.

Supplementary Materials: Include additional resources like library books, field trips, and community resources.

Organize Curriculum Content

Scope and Sequence: Outline the scope (what will be covered) and sequence (the order in which it will be taught) for each subject.

Weekly/Monthly Plans: Break down the curriculum into weekly or monthly plans to manage pacing and ensure coverage of all topics.

Document Format

Document: Use a word processor (e.g., Microsoft Word, Google Docs) to create a curriculum guide with sections for each subject and grade level.

Digital Format: Use spreadsheet software (e.g., Google Sheets) for a visual representation of the scope and sequence. Online curriculum platforms can also be used to organize and track progress.

Creating a Lesson Plan

Define Learning Objectives

Specific Goals: Identify specific learning objectives for each lesson that align with the overall curriculum goals.

Plan Activities and Materials

Lesson Activities: Design engaging activities and assignments that help achieve the learning objectives (e.g., reading assignments, experiments, group work).

Materials Needed: List the materials and resources required for each lesson.

Develop Assessment Methods

Formative Assessments: Plan for ongoing assessments such as quizzes, informal observations, or class discussions.

Summative Assessments: Include final assessments like tests, projects, or presentations to evaluate overall understanding.

Create a Lesson Plan Template

Lesson Plan Template: Use a consistent format for each lesson plan, including sections for objectives, activities, materials, and assessments.

Document Format: Create lesson plans in a word processor or use a lesson planning app to organize and store plans digitally.

Document Format

Document: Create individual lesson plan documents using a word processor, saving them in a structured folder system.

Digital Format: Use online lesson planning tools (e.g., Google Classroom, Planbook) to create, store, and share lesson plans.

Creating Projects

Define Project Objectives

Learning Goals: Determine what students should learn or demonstrate through the project.

Plan the Project

Project Outline: Design a project that includes clear instructions, goals, and evaluation criteria.

Materials and Resources: List materials needed and provide access to any additional resources.

Develop a Timeline

Project Schedule: Create a timeline for project milestones, including research, development, and presentation phases.

Assess the Project

Rubric: Develop a rubric or assessment criteria to evaluate the project's success based on the defined objectives.

Document Format

Document: Use a word processor or spreadsheet to create and store project guidelines, rubrics, and schedules.

Digital Format: Utilize project management tools (e.g., Trello, Asana) to organize and track project progress.

Maintaining a Portfolio

Define Portfolio Content

Student Work: Include samples of student work, such as assignments, projects, tests, and creative work.

Assessments and Reflections: Add records of assessments and student reflections on their learning progress.

Organize the Portfolio

Sectioning: Create sections for each subject or grade level, and organize work chronologically or by topic.

Labeling: Clearly label each section and document for easy reference.

Update Regularly

Ongoing Maintenance: Regularly update the portfolio with new work and assessments. Ensure that it reflects the student's progress over time.

Document Format

Physical Portfolio: Use a binder with plastic sleeves to store physical copies of student work.

Digital Portfolio: Create a digital portfolio using cloud storage (e.g., Google Drive) or specialized portfolio platforms (e.g., Seesaw). Organize files in folders by subject and grade level.

Review and Reflect

Periodic Reviews: Regularly review the portfolio to assess progress and identify areas for improvement. Use it as a tool for student self reflection and goal setting.

Understanding Differentiation

What is Differentiation?

Definition: Differentiation involves adjusting teaching methods, materials, and assessments to accommodate the varied learning styles, abilities, and interests of students.

Purpose: It aims to ensure all students can engage with the content and make progress, regardless of their starting point or learning preferences.

Differentiating Lesson Plans

Identify Learning Objectives

GradeLevel Goals: Determine the key learning objectives for each child based on their grade level and individual needs.

Skill Levels: Assess each child's current skill levels and tailor objectives accordingly.

Design Flexible Activities

Tiered Assignments: Create tiered assignments with varying levels of complexity. For example, provide basic, intermediate, and advanced versions of a task to accommodate different skill levels.

Choice Boards: Use choice boards or menus that offer different types of activities. Allow children to select tasks that align with their interests and abilities.

Utilize Varied Instructional Strategies

Visual Aids: Incorporate visual aids, such as charts and diagrams, for visual learners.

HandsOn Activities: Include hands-on or kinesthetic activities for children who learn best through movement and manipulation.

Verbal Instruction: Offer clear, verbal instructions and discussions for auditory learners.

Adapt Assessments

Flexible Assessment Methods: Use different assessment methods, such as oral presentations, written reports, or creative projects, to evaluate learning based on each child's strengths.

Rubrics: Develop rubrics with criteria tailored to different skill levels to fairly assess student work.

Document Format

Lesson Plan Template: Use a lesson plan template that includes sections for differentiated activities, materials, and assessments. Adapt it for each child's needs.

Digital Tools: Utilize digital lesson planning tools (e.g., Google Docs, Trello) to create and manage differentiated lesson plans.

Differentiating Unit Studies

Plan the Unit Study

Unit Goals: Define the overall goals and objectives for the unit study that align with your curriculum and the children's grade levels.

Thematic Approach: Choose a central theme or topic that is relevant and engaging for all children.

Design Differentiated Components

Content: Provide content at varying levels of difficulty. For example, use different reading materials, videos, or resources that cater to each child's comprehension level.

Activities: Develop a range of activities that address different learning styles. Include options for independent work, group projects, and hands on experiences.

Group and Individual Work

Flexible Grouping: Group children based on their abilities or interests for certain activities. Rotate groups to provide diverse collaborative experiences.

Individualized Tasks: Assign individual tasks that cater to each child's interests and skill levels while still aligning with the unit's overall objectives.

Assess and Reflect

Ongoing Assessment: Use formative assessments throughout the unit to monitor progress and make adjustments as needed.

Reflective Discussions: Include opportunities for children to reflect on what they have learned and share their experiences.

Document Format

Unit Study Binder: Create a binder or digital folder for each unit study, including sections for differentiated activities, materials, and assessments.

Online Platforms: Use online platforms (e.g., Google Classroom) to organize and share unit study materials and assignments.

Implementing Differentiation in a Homeschool Setting

Create a Flexible Schedule

Adjustable Timetable: Design a flexible schedule that allows for different paces and needs. Allocate time for individual work and group activities.

Rotation: Rotate between subjects and activities to ensure all children receive attention and support.

Monitor and Adapt

Regular CheckIns: Regularly check in with each child to assess their understanding and adjust instruction as needed.

Feedback: Provide constructive feedback and make adjustments based on each child's progress and needs.

Foster Independence

SelfPaced Learning: Encourage self paced learning where possible, allowing children to work at their own speed while meeting overall objectives.

Goal Setting: Help children set personal learning goals and track their progress.

By implementing these strategies, you can effectively differentiate instruction to meet the needs of multiple children in your homeschool, ensuring that each child receives a personalized and engaging learning experience.

Understanding Asynchrony in Neurodivergent and Gifted Students

What is Asynchrony?

Definition

Asynchrony refers to the uneven development of a child's cognitive, emotional, and physical abilities. This phenomenon is particularly common in neurodivergent individuals, including those who are gifted.

Characteristics

Advanced Skills: A child may show advanced abilities in one or more areas (e.g., intellectual, creative, or academic skills).

Lagging Skills: Simultaneously, the child may be developmentally behind or on par with peers in other areas (e.g., social skills, emotional regulation, or other academic subjects).

Asynchrony in Neurodivergent and Gifted Students

Common Patterns

Gifted Students: Often excel in areas of strength such as problem solving, creativity, or specific academic subjects while exhibiting delays in social skills or executive functioning.

Neurodivergent Students: May experience differences in cognitive processing, leading to asynchronous development in various domains. For example, a child with dyslexia might be exceptionally talented in mathematics but struggle with reading.

Causes

Cognitive Differences: Variations in brain development and functioning.

Educational Environment: Differences in educational opportunities or teaching methods.

Emotional and Social Factors: Challenges in emotional regulation or social interactions.

Addressing Asynchrony

Recognize and Validate

Acknowledge Differences: Understand that asynchrony is a natural part of development for many neurodivergent and gifted students.

Validation: Validate the child's strengths and challenges without overemphasizing deficits.

Provide Targeted Support

Tailored Instruction: Offer differentiated instruction that caters to the child's strengths and areas for growth.

Support Strategies: Implement strategies and tools that address specific developmental needs, such as social skills training or executive functioning supports.

Foster Strengths

Leverage Strengths: Encourage and nurture the child's advanced skills to build confidence and self efficacy.

Engagement: Engage the child in activities and projects that align with their strengths to promote motivation and a positive self image.

Maintain Balance

Balanced Approach: Provide support for areas where the child is lagging while continuing to challenge and develop their advanced skills.

Integrated Learning: Integrate learning activities that bridge strengths and challenges, promoting overall growth.

Building SelfEfficacy and SelfEsteem

Encourage Achievement

Celebrate Successes: Recognize and celebrate achievements in both advanced areas and areas of improvement.

Set Goals: Help the child set realistic, attainable goals to foster a sense of accomplishment and progress.

Provide Emotional Support

Empathy and Understanding: Offer emotional support and understanding, acknowledging the challenges and frustrations the child may face.

Resilience Building: Teach resilience and coping strategies to help the child navigate difficulties and setbacks.

Promote Positive SelfImage

Affirmative Feedback: Provide constructive feedback that focuses on effort and growth.

Encourage Autonomy: Support the child's independence and self direction in learning, allowing them to take ownership of their strengths and challenges.

Model Growth Mindset

Growth Mindset: Model and teach a growth mindset, emphasizing that abilities and intelligence can be developed through effort and perseverance.

Learning from Challenges: Encourage viewing challenges as opportunities for learning and growth rather than as failures.

Practical Application for Parents

Observe and Assess

Regular Observations: Regularly observe and assess the child's development across different domains to understand their unique pattern of asynchrony.

Professional Input: Seek professional assessments if needed to gain insights into the child's cognitive and emotional development.

Create an Individualized Plan

Custom Learning Plan: Develop an individualized learning plan that addresses both strengths and areas for improvement.

Flexible Adjustments: Be flexible and willing to adjust the plan based on the child's evolving needs and progress.

Encourage Open Communication

Family Discussions: Have open discussions with the child about their experiences, strengths, and challenges to build trust and understanding.

Collaborative Approach: Work collaboratively with educators, therapists, and other professionals to provide comprehensive support.

By understanding and addressing asynchrony, parents can effectively support their neurodivergent or gifted children, fostering a positive and balanced learning experience that values both their strengths and areas of growth.

What is a Unit Study?

Definition of a Unit Study

Unit Study: A unit study is an integrated approach to teaching that focuses on a single topic or theme, incorporating multiple subjects and skills into one cohesive learning experience. It aims to explore a topic in depth from various perspectives, connecting different areas of study in a meaningful way.

Components of a Unit Study

Central Theme: A central topic or theme around which all subjects and activities are organized.

Interdisciplinary Learning: Integration of multiple subjects, such as language arts, math, science, and history, into the study of the central theme.

HandsOn Activities: Engaging, handson projects and activities that reinforce the theme and make learning interactive.

Why Use a Unit Study in a Humane Homeschool?

Holistic Learning Approach

Integrated Learning: A unit study provides a comprehensive understanding of a topic by linking various subjects together. For example, studying the topic of "space" might include reading about space exploration, writing a report on planets, solving math problems related to distance and scale, conducting science experiments, and learning about the history of space travel.

RealWorld Connections: This approach helps students see the connections between different areas of knowledge, making learning more relevant and engaging.

Encourages Depth of Understanding

InDepth Exploration: By focusing on one topic, students can explore it in depth, fostering a deeper understanding and retention of information.

Critical Thinking: Students are encouraged to think critically about how different disciplines intersect and contribute to their understanding of the topic.

Engages Multiple Learning Styles

Varied Activities: Unit studies often include a variety of activities (e.g., reading, writing, projects, experiments) that cater to different learning styles and preferences.

HandsOn Learning: Activities like experiments, field trips, and creative projects appeal to kinesthetic learners and help make abstract concepts more concrete.

Promotes Active Learning

StudentCentered: Students take an active role in their learning, engaging with the material in a way that interests them.

Creativity and Exploration: Encourages creativity and exploration, allowing students to approach the topic from multiple angles and develop their own interests within the theme.

Builds Stronger Connections

Contextual Learning: Helps students build connections between different subjects and understand how knowledge is interconnected.

Enhanced Retention: When students learn about a topic from multiple perspectives, they are more likely to retain and apply the information.

Implementing a Unit Study in a Humane Homeschool

Planning the Unit Study

Choose a Theme: Select a central theme that is broad enough to encompass various subjects but focused enough to provide depth. Examples include "Ancient Egypt," "The Environment," or "Inventions."

Set Objectives: Define clear learning objectives for each subject area related to the theme. For instance, in a unit study on "Ancient Egypt," objectives might include understanding Egyptian culture (history), learning about hieroglyphics (language arts), exploring the geography of Egypt (science), and analyzing Egyptian artifacts (math).

Designing Integrated Activities

Language Arts: Include reading materials related to the theme, writing assignments such as reports or creative stories, and vocabulary development.

Math: Create math problems or projects that relate to the theme. For example, calculating the dimensions of pyramids or analyzing ancient Egyptian trade.

Science: Conduct experiments or investigations related to the theme. For example, exploring the Nile River's ecosystem or building models of ancient Egyptian inventions.

History: Study historical aspects related to the theme, such as significant events, cultures, and figures. Include timelines, biographies, and historical analysis.

Art and Music: Integrate artistic and musical activities that reflect the theme, such as creating art inspired by the theme or studying music from the relevant period.

Organizing the Unit Study

Create a Schedule: Develop a schedule that outlines when and how each subject will be covered within the unit. Include time for individual work, group projects, and assessments.

Document Progress: Maintain records of activities, assignments, and assessments. Use a portfolio to showcase completed work and reflections.

Assessing and Reflecting

Assess Understanding: Use various assessment methods (e.g., quizzes, projects, presentations) to evaluate student understanding of the theme.

Reflect on Learning: Encourage students to reflect on what they have learned and how different subjects are interconnected.

Adapting and Adjusting

Flexible Approach: Be prepared to adapt the unit study based on student interests, needs, and progress. Adjust activities and materials as necessary to enhance engagement and learning outcomes.

By incorporating a unit study approach, a humane homeschool can provide a rich, interdisciplinary learning experience that connects different subjects in a meaningful way, respects diverse learning styles, and fosters a deeper understanding of the material.

What is Multisensory Learning?

Definition

Multisensory Learning: An educational approach that engages multiple senses (sight, sound, touch, taste, and smell) to enhance learning and memory. It integrates various sensory modalities to reinforce concepts and make learning more engaging and effective.

Neuroscience Behind Multisensory Learning

Memory Consolidation: Neuroscience research supports that multisensory experiences can improve the transfer of information from short term to long term memory. Engaging multiple senses creates richer and more robust neural connections, making it easier for the brain to store and retrieve information.

Enhanced Brain Activity: When multiple senses are involved, different areas of the brain are activated, leading to increased neural pathways and more effective processing of information.

Increased Engagement: Multisensory learning can increase student engagement and motivation by catering to diverse learning styles and preferences.

Benefits of Multisensory Learning for Neurodivergent Students

Supports Diverse Learning Needs

Movement Integration: For students who need to move during lessons, multisensory learning can incorporate physical activities, such as using manipulatives, moving around the room, or engaging in handson projects. This helps maintain focus and engagement.

Varied Sensory Input: Engaging multiple senses can benefit neurodivergent students by accommodating different sensory processing preferences and needs, making learning more accessible and enjoyable.

Personalized Learning

InterestBased Activities: Tailoring multisensory activities to a child's interests and preferences can enhance motivation and make learning more relevant. For example, if a child is interested in animals, incorporating sensory rich activities related to animal studies can improve engagement and retention.

Reinforcing Learning

Targeted Activities: Multisensory activities can reinforce concepts through repetition and varied sensory input. For instance, a student might learn about fractions using visual aids, physical manipulatives, and auditory explanations, which together strengthen understanding.

Using Multisensory Learning in a Unit Study

Incorporating Multisensory Elements

Visual: Use charts, diagrams, videos, and illustrations to present information. Visual aids can help clarify concepts and provide context.

Auditory: Include discussions, storytelling, and audio recordings related to the unit theme. Listening to relevant content can reinforce learning and aid comprehension.

Kinesthetic: Engage students in handson activities, experiments, and movement based learning. For example, building models, conducting science experiments, or acting out historical events can make learning interactive.

Tactile: Use materials that students can touch and manipulate, such as textures, sensory bins, or craft supplies. Tactile experiences can help solidify abstract concepts.

Integrating Arts and Crafts

Arts and Crafts: Incorporate arts and crafts into the unit study to maintain interest and motivation. For instance, creating posters, dioramas, or models related to the unit theme can provide a creative outlet and reinforce learning.

Handicrafts: Utilize handicrafts as a way to explore and express learning. For example, making historical artifacts or designing visual representations of scientific concepts can enhance understanding and retention.

Designing Engaging Activities

ProjectBased Learning: Plan projects that integrate multiple senses and subjects. For instance, a unit study on ecosystems might include creating a habitat diorama, writing a report, and conducting a related science experiment.

Interactive Stations: Set up learning stations that focus on different sensory modalities. Each station might cover a different aspect of the unit study, allowing students to engage with the material in various ways.

Adapting to Student Needs

Flexible Approach: Be flexible and responsive to the needs of each student. Adjust multisensory activities based on individual preferences and learning styles to ensure that all students benefit from the approach.

Feedback and Reflection: Encourage students to provide feedback on the multisensory activities and reflect on what works best for them. This can help tailor future activities to better support their learning needs.

Example of a Multisensory Unit Study

Language

Subject: Phonemic Awareness and Vocabulary Development

Activity: Sound Wall Creation

Visual: Create a sound wall where each section represents a specific phoneme or sound. Use visual symbols or images to illustrate each sound, such as pictures of items that start with that sound.

Auditory: Introduce and practice the sounds through auditory activities like sound matching games, where students listen to and identify different phonemes.

Kinesthetic: Engage students in handson activities, such as moving letter tiles or tokens to the appropriate sections on the sound wall based on the sound they hear.

Tactile: Use textured materials to create the sound wall (e.g., fabric for different sounds), allowing students to feel the different sections as they work with phonemes.

By using a sound wall, students can develop a deeper understanding of phonemic awareness and improve their reading and language skills through structured literacy practices.

Speaking

Subject: Oral Presentation Skills

Activity: Planet Report Presentation

Visual: Students create a visual aid, such as a poster or slide presentation, about their chosen planet.

Auditory: Practice delivering the report aloud, focusing on clear speech and engaging storytelling techniques.

Kinesthetic: Use props related to the topic (e.g., a model of the planet) during the presentation.

Tactile: Incorporate hands on demonstrations, such as showing a model of the planet, to enhance the presentation.

Reading

Subject: Comprehension and Analysis

Activity: Story Mapping

Visual: Read a story related to the unit and create a visual map of the plot with illustrations and labels.

Auditory: Discuss the story's themes and plot points in a group discussion.

Kinesthetic: Act out parts of the story or create a physical timeline of events.

Tactile: Use tactile materials (e.g., felt pieces) to create a story map that students can manipulate.

Writing

Subject: Creative Writing

Activity: Story Creation

Visual: Write and illustrate a story related to the unit theme (e.g., a fictional adventure on another planet).

Auditory: Read the story aloud to practice fluency and expression.

Kinesthetic: Use movement to brainstorm and plan the story, such as acting out scenes or using a large story map on the floor.

Tactile: Incorporate textured paper or other materials into the writing process to enhance the sensory experience.

Math

Subject: Fractions

Activity: Fraction Pizza

Visual: Create a "pizza" using paper plates or cardboard, divided into different fraction slices.

Auditory: Discuss and explain fractions using terms like halves, quarters, and eighths.

Kinesthetic: Have students physically cut the pizza into fractions and rearrange the slices to understand the concept.

Tactile: Use real or felt materials to make the pizza and its slices for a handson experience.

Unit Theme: "The Solar System"

Visual Activities

Create a Solar System Poster: Students design a poster depicting the solar system, using drawings and labels for each planet.

Watch Educational Videos: View videos that explain the solar system's structure and function.

Auditory Activities

Listen to a Podcast: Find a podcast about space exploration and discuss key points.

Song and Rhyme: Use a song or rhyme to help memorize the names and order of the planets.

Kinesthetic Activities

Build a Model: Construct a 3D model of the solar system using craft materials.

Planet Walk: Create a scale model of the solar system in the backyard or classroom, with students walking to represent the distance between planets.

Tactile Activities

Texture Book: Create a tactile book with different textures representing various planets.

Sensory Bin: Fill a bin with items representing space (e.g., glitter for stars) and let students explore.

Arts and Crafts

Planet Crafts: Make planet models using clay or papermâché.

Space Art: Create artwork inspired by the solar system, such as paintings or collages.

By incorporating multisensory learning into a unit study, parents can create a dynamic and engaging educational experience that supports various learning styles, enhances memory retention, and keeps students motivated.

History

Subject: Ancient Civilizations

Activity: Ancient Egypt Diorama

Visual: Create a diorama depicting a scene from Ancient Egypt, using miniature figures and materials.

Auditory: Listen to a historical overview or story about Ancient Egypt.

Kinesthetic: Assemble and decorate the diorama using handson crafting materials.

Tactile: Use different textures (e.g., sand for desert) in the diorama to bring the scene to life.

Art

Subject: Impressionist Painting

Activity: Create an Impressionist Painting

Visual: Study famous Impressionist paintings and use them as inspiration.

Auditory: Listen to music that reflects the Impressionist era to set the mood.

Kinesthetic: Use various painting techniques, such as dabbing and blending, to mimic the Impressionist style.

Tactile: Experiment with different brushes and textures to create a painting with varied sensory experiences.

Music

Subject: Rhythm and Beat

Activity: Rhythm Patterns with Instruments

Visual: Use visual aids like rhythm charts or patterns to demonstrate different beats.

Auditory: Listen to and practice clapping or playing different rhythmic patterns using musical instruments.

Kinesthetic: Move to the rhythm or use body percussion to feel the beat physically.

Tactile: Experiment with different instruments or materials to produce various sounds and rhythms.

By incorporating multisensory activities into each subject area, a humane homeschool can create a rich and engaging learning environment that supports diverse learning styles and enhances overall educational outcomes.

Embracing Diversity in Homeschooling: Avoiding Comparison and Fostering Community Collaboration

Comparison Is the Thief of Joy

It's natural to feel tempted to compare your homeschooling journey to others, but it's important to recognize that comparison can undermine the joy and satisfaction you derive from your unique educational approach. Each homeschool is as distinct as the families behind it—no two are exactly the same, just as no two students or parents are. The way one family structures their homeschool might not work for another, and that's perfectly okay.

Value Diversity

Homeschooling is a highly personalized endeavor. What works brilliantly for one student might not be suitable for another, and that's a strength rather than a limitation. Each family brings its own values, interests, and needs to the homeschooling experience. Embrace this diversity, knowing that your homeschool is tailored to fit your child's individual learning style, strengths, and challenges.

Community Collaboration

While your homeschool should be a reflection of your family's unique needs, collaborating with a community of homeschoolers can provide valuable support and resources. Consider working with local or online communities to build a resource center where families can exchange information and materials.

Local Libraries: Partner with local libraries to create a community resource hub. Libraries often have meeting spaces and can help organize events, workshops, and resource exchanges for homeschooling families.

Churches and Community Centers: Reach out to local churches or community centers to establish a resource center. These locations can serve as gathering spots for group activities, classes, and resource sharing.

Small Businesses: Collaborate with trusted local businesses to support your homeschool community. Small businesses can sometimes offer discounts, materials, or space for educational activities.

Online Platforms: Utilize online forums, social media groups, and virtual communities to connect with other homeschool families. Online platforms can facilitate the exchange of ideas, resources, and support on a broader scale.

Building a Resource Center

A community resource center, whether physical or virtual, can become a valuable asset for homeschooling families.

Identify Needs: Assess the needs of your local homeschooling community to determine what resources and support would be most beneficial.

Gather Resources: Collect educational materials, books, and tools that families can borrow or access. Consider including a range of subjects and grade levels.

Organize Events: Host workshops, seminars, or social events to foster collaboration and skill sharing among homeschooling families.

Promote Inclusivity: Ensure that the resource center is welcoming to all families, regardless of their educational philosophy or background.

By focusing on the strengths and needs of your own homeschool while embracing the diversity and collaboration offered by a supportive community, you can create a fulfilling and effective educational experience for your child. Avoiding comparison and celebrating the uniqueness of each homeschooling journey will help you find joy and satisfaction in your personalized educational approach.

Managing Health and Wellness in a Humane Homeschool

Parent as a Home School Nurse Responsibilities

Health Monitoring and First Aid

Basic Care: As the primary caregiver and educator, you are responsible for monitoring your child's health and addressing minor injuries or illnesses. This includes providing first aid for cuts, bruises, and other minor ailments.

Health Records: Maintain records of your child's health, including vaccination schedules, medical history, and any medications administered. This helps ensure that all health needs are met and provides valuable information for health professionals if needed.

Managing School Days and Appointments

Making Up Missed School Days

Flexibility: Develop a flexible approach to scheduling to accommodate for unexpected illnesses or appointments. If a child misses school due to health reasons, adjust the schedule to make up for lost instructional time without causing additional stress.

CatchUp Strategies: Implement strategies for catching up on missed work, such as reviewing missed lessons, providing additional practice, or utilizing online resources to supplement learning.

Doctor's Appointments and Physicals

Routine CheckUps: Schedule regular physical exams and dental checkups to ensure your child's health and development are on track. Include these appointments in your planning to minimize disruptions to the educational schedule.

Documentation: Keep documentation of all medical appointments and physicals. This can be useful for tracking health trends and ensuring that all necessary health screenings are completed.

Maintaining Healthy Sleep, Nutrition, and Exercise

AgeAppropriate Sleep Requirements

Sleep Guidelines: Adhere to recommended sleep guidelines based on age. For example, younger children generally need 1012 hours of sleep per night, while teenagers typically need 810 hours.

Consistent Routine: Establish a consistent sleep routine to promote healthy sleep patterns. This includes setting regular bedtimes and wake up times, and creating a relaxing bedtime environment.

Balanced Nutrition

Healthy Diet: Provide a balanced diet that includes a variety of nutrients to support your child's growth and learning. This involves incorporating fruits, vegetables, whole grains, lean proteins, and healthy fats into daily meals.

Meal Planning: Plan and prepare meals that meet nutritional needs and accommodate any dietary restrictions or preferences. Involve children in meal planning and preparation to encourage healthy eating habits.

Regular Exercise

Physical Activity: Ensure that your child engages in regular physical activity appropriate for their age. For younger children, this might include playtime, outdoor activities, and structured exercise. For older children and teens, encourage participation in sports, fitness classes, or other physical activities.

Incorporate Movement: Integrate movement into the daily routine. For example, include short physical breaks during study sessions, or plan active outings such as hikes or bike rides.

Balancing Health with Education

Integrated Approach

Holistic WellBeing: Recognize that health and education are interconnected. A healthy lifestyle supports cognitive function, emotional wellbeing, and overall academic performance.

Adaptations: Make adjustments to the educational plan as needed based on health considerations. For instance, if a child is recovering from an illness, provide flexible deadlines or modified assignments to accommodate their needs.

Supporting Healthy Development

Developmental Needs

AgeAppropriate Care: Tailor health and wellness practices to the developmental stage of your child. For example, early childhood may require more focus on establishing routines and habits, while adolescence may involve supporting independence and managing stress.

Education on Health: Educate children about the importance of healthy habits and self care as they grow older. Encourage them to take responsibility for their own health and wellbeing in age appropriate ways.

By managing these aspects effectively, parents can ensure that their child's health and educational needs are well balanced, supporting a positive and productive homeschooling experience.

The Spectrum of Homeschooling: From HighBudget to BudgetFriendly

HighBudget Humane Homeschool

Curriculum and Resources:

Invest in premium, comprehensive curricula that include interactive digital platforms, professional development courses, and specialized materials for diverse subjects.

Purchase high quality textbooks, workbooks, and educational software from reputable publishers.

Subscribe to educational apps and online learning platforms that offer personalized learning experiences and real time feedback.

Learning Environment:

Create a dedicated, well equipped learning space with ergonomic furniture, a variety of learning materials, and advanced technology such as tablets or laptops.

Set up a home library with a wide selection of books, reference materials, and educational games.

Extracurricular Activities:

Enroll students in enrichment programs, such as coding camps, art classes, or music lessons, offered by professionals in your area.

Facilitate regular field trips to museums, science centers, and cultural events.

Community and Support:

Join or form exclusive homeschooling coops or groups that offer additional resources, workshops, and networking opportunities.

MidRange Humane Homeschool

Curriculum and Resources:

Opt for well reviewed, midrange curricula that offer a balance between cost and quality, including some digital components or supplementary materials.

Use library resources and free or affordable online educational resources to supplement learning.

Learning Environment:

Set up a functional and organized learning area with basic educational supplies, such as desks, chairs, and storage solutions.

Invest in a few key educational tools and resources, like a good set of reference books and art supplies.

Extracurricular Activities:

Participate in community based programs, such as local sports teams, clubs, or arts programs, that offer affordable or free activities.

Plan occasional field trips to local educational sites, parks, or community events.

Community and Support:

Connect with local homeschooling groups or online communities for resource sharing and support. Attend workshops or support meetings that are low cost or free.

BudgetFriendly Humane Homeschool

Curriculum and Resources:

Utilize free or low cost educational resources, such as open educational resources (OER), free online courses, and public domain books.

Create your own curriculum using free templates, lesson plans, and materials available online.

Learning Environment:

Set up a simple and functional learning space using repurposed furniture and materials from thrift stores or donations.

Use everyday household items for hands on learning activities, such as DIY science experiments or math games.

Extracurricular Activities:

Take advantage of free community resources, such as local parks, public libraries, and community centers, for educational and recreational activities.

Explore free or low cost online classes, educational videos, and interactive learning tools.

Community and Support:

Engage with local or online homeschooling support groups to exchange ideas, resources, and advice. Participate in free community events and parentled coops.

Key Takeaways for a Humane Homeschool

Adaptability: A humane homeschool is adaptable to various financial situations. It focuses on the quality of education and the wellbeing of the student rather than the cost of materials.

Creativity: Use creativity to maximize resources. Many valuable educational experiences do not require significant financial investment.

Community: Leveraging community resources and connections can provide support and enrich the homeschooling experience regardless of budget.

By understanding that humane homeschooling can be effectively implemented at any income level, parents can tailor their approach to fit their financial situation while still providing a supportive and nurturing educational environment.

Valuing Lifelong Learning in a Humane Homeschool

In a humane homeschool, lifelong learning is not just a goal for students but a core value embraced by the entire family. This approach acknowledges that learning is a continuous, dynamic process that extends beyond formal education and involves everyone—from parents to students.

Embracing a Culture of Curiosity

For All Ages: Lifelong learning means cultivating curiosity and a love for discovery at every stage of life. Parents model this behavior by pursuing their own interests, exploring new skills, and engaging in personal growth, thus demonstrating that learning is a lifelong endeavor.

Encouraging Exploration: Students are encouraged to follow their passions, ask questions, and seek out new knowledge in areas that interest them. This approach fosters an intrinsic motivation to learn and discover, rather than viewing education as a series of tasks to be completed.

Integrating Learning into Daily Life

Learning Everywhere: In a humane homeschool, learning extends beyond traditional educational settings. Families view everyday activities and environments as opportunities for education. Whether it's cooking, gardening, traveling, or visiting local events, these experiences are seen as valuable learning moments.

RealWorld Applications: By integrating learning into real life situations, families can connect academic concepts with practical experiences. For example, a family trip might involve exploring geography, history, and cultural studies, while a home project might cover mathematics, science, and engineering principles.

Adopting John Holt's Perspective on Unschooling

Learning Through Living: John Holt, a prominent advocate for unschooling, emphasized that learning happens naturally when children are immersed in real life experiences just like a scientist. He believed that when children are free to explore their interests and engage with the world around them, they learn more effectively than through structured education alone.

Seeing Environment as a Classroom: Holt's approach encourages families to view their environment as a classroom. This perspective means that every interaction, observation, and activity can be an opportunity for learning. Families can create a rich, stimulating learning environment by embracing the world as a source of knowledge.

Fostering a Collaborative Learning Environment

Shared Learning Experiences: Lifelong learning is a collaborative process in a humane homeschool. Families learn together through discussions, projects, and shared activities. This collaboration not only strengthens family bonds but also creates a supportive environment where everyone can contribute their knowledge and skills.

Adapting to Change: Lifelong learners are adaptable and open to new ideas. Families in a humane homeschool embrace change and evolving interests, allowing their educational approach to adapt to their needs and experiences.

Supporting Personal Growth

Encouraging Personal Interests: Each family member is supported in pursuing their personal interests and goals. Whether it's a parent learning a new craft or a child exploring a new hobby, this support reinforces the idea that learning is a personal and ongoing journey.

Reflecting and Evolving: Families regularly reflect on their learning experiences and adjust their approaches as needed. This reflective practice helps to continuously improve and adapt the learning environment to better meet everyone's needs.

A humane homeschool values lifelong learning by fostering a culture of curiosity and exploration that involves every family member. By viewing everyday experiences as learning opportunities and embracing John Holt's perspective on unschooling, families can integrate education into all aspects of life. This approach not only enhances the educational experience but also enriches family life, demonstrating that learning is a continuous, shared journey that extends well beyond traditional schooling.

Understanding Social Cognitive Learning Theory, Mirror Neurons, and Autodidacticism

Social Cognitive Learning Theory

Concept Overview: Social Cognitive Learning Theory, developed by Albert Bandura (*a professional who left behaviorism behind*), emphasizes the role of observation, imitation, and modeling in learning. According to this theory, people learn by observing others and imitating their behavior, attitudes, and emotional reactions. It integrates cognitive, behavioral, and environmental factors, recognizing that learning occurs in a social context.

Role of Observation: In a homeschooling environment, parents and educators are key models for students. Children learn not just from direct instruction but also by observing how adults approach problems, manage emotions, and engage with learning. This process of modeling helps students develop cognitive and behavioral skills.

Mirror Neurons and Their Impact

Understanding Mirror Neurons: Mirror neurons are brain cells that activate both when an individual performs an action and when they observe someone else performing the same action. These neurons play a crucial role in empathy, imitation, and learning by observation.

Connection to Learning: Mirror neurons support social cognitive learning by enabling individuals to understand and mimic others' behaviors. This neural mechanism helps students learn through observation, making it important for parents to model desired behaviors and learning strategies effectively.

Gradual Release of Responsibility

Concept Explained: The gradual release of responsibility is an instructional strategy where the teacher gradually shifts the responsibility of learning from the teacher to the student. It involves a sequence of steps: I do (modeling), We do (guided practice), and You do (independent practice).

Application in Homeschooling: Parents use this approach to scaffold learning, starting with direct instruction and progressively allowing students to take more responsibility for their learning. This method helps build students' confidence and independence while ensuring they receive the support they need.

Supporting Autodidacts and Balancing Learning

Autodidacticism Defined: An autodidact is a self taught individual who takes the initiative to learn independently. Autodidacts are often motivated, self directed learners who pursue knowledge outside of formal educational settings.

Recognizing Autodidacts: In a homeschooling environment, some students may show characteristics of autodidacts, such as pursuing personal interests with minimal guidance or seeking out resources independently.

Balancing Support: While supporting an autodidact's learning, parents must ensure that their educational needs are not neglected. This balance involves:

Providing Resources: Offer access to materials and resources that align with the student's interests and learning goals while ensuring they meet educational standards.

Guiding Without Overstepping: Allow students to lead their learning process, but provide guidance and feedback to ensure they are meeting educational objectives and not missing critical skills or knowledge.

Regular CheckIns: Schedule regular check ins to assess progress, address any gaps in knowledge, and adjust support as needed.

Preparing for Independent Learning

Skills for Independence: The ultimate goal of fostering autodidactic skills is to prepare students for higher education or the workforce, where self directed learning becomes crucial. Developing skills such as time management, goal setting, and resourcefulness is essential.

Encouraging SelfReliance: Support students in setting their own learning goals, finding resources, and evaluating their progress. This prepares them for the independence required in college or a professional environment.

Social Cognitive Learning Theory and the concept of mirror neurons highlight the importance of observation and modeling in learning. Gradual release of responsibility is a key strategy in transitioning from direct instruction to independent learning. For students who are autodidacts or self taught, parents should balance support with encouraging autonomy, ensuring that educational needs are met while fostering independence. By understanding and applying these concepts, parents can effectively guide their children toward becoming self reliant learners prepared for future academic and professional success.

Managing the Start of a School Year, Scheduling, and Pacing in a Humane Homeschool

Starting the School Year

Preparation and Planning:

Review State Requirements: Before the school year begins, review your state's homeschooling laws and instructional hour requirements. Ensure you understand what is required in terms of subjects, hours, and documentation.

Set Goals: Establish educational goals for the year based on your child's needs, strengths, and interests. Include both academic and personal development goals.

Gather Resources: Collect and organize all necessary materials, such as textbooks, workbooks, digital resources, and supplies. Prepare any curriculum materials and plan out initial lessons.

Create a Warm and Welcoming Environment:

Set Up a Learning Space: Designate a dedicated learning space that is conducive to studying and free from distractions. Involve your child in setting up this space to make it engaging and personal.

Establish Routines: Develop a consistent daily routine that includes time for lessons, breaks, and extracurricular activities. Consistency helps create a sense of stability and predictability.

Determining a Schedule

Traditional Schedule vs. Block Schedule:

Traditional Schedule: This involves a standard school day with set times for different subjects. For example, Math from 910 AM, Language Arts from 1011 AM, etc.

Block Schedule: This approach groups subjects into longer, less frequent periods. For example, instead of daily 45 minute periods, you might have a 90 minute block for Math and Science on Mondays and Wednesdays, and Language Arts and Social Studies on Tuesdays and Thursdays. Block scheduling can allow for more in depth exploration of subjects and may reduce daily transitions.

Adhering to Instructional Hour Requirements:

Check Requirements: Ensure that your schedule meets your state's required instructional hours. This often includes a minimum number of hours per day and days per year.

Track Hours: Keep accurate records of instructional hours to ensure compliance. Document daily or weekly hours spent on each subject.

Pacing Lessons and Curriculum

Setting a Pace:

Curriculum Scope: Review your curriculum to understand the scope and sequence. Break down the curriculum into manageable units or modules.

Create a Plan: Develop a pacing guide that outlines what should be covered each week or month. Allow flexibility for revisiting challenging topics or exploring areas of particular interest.

Monitor Progress: Regularly assess your child's understanding and adjust the pace as needed. Use informal assessments, such as quizzes or projects, and formal assessments, if applicable.

Balancing Flexibility and Structure:

Adaptability: Be prepared to adjust the schedule and pacing based on your child's progress and needs. Flexibility allows you to address any challenges and capitalize on opportunities for deeper learning.

Scheduled Reviews: Periodically review your child's progress and the effectiveness of the schedule. Make necessary adjustments to ensure that learning goals are being met.

Choosing Between School Year and YearRound Schooling

Traditional School Year:

Advantages: Aligns with the typical academic calendar, with a long summer break. It can be easier to coordinate with extracurricular activities and social events.

Disadvantages: Students may experience a "summer slide" where they lose some of what they learned during the break. It may also require more intensive review at the start of each year.

YearRound Schooling:

Advantages: Provides continuous learning with shorter, more frequent breaks throughout the year. It can reduce the summer slide and keep students engaged year round.

Disadvantages: May require more planning to coordinate with family vacations and community activities. It might also be less conventional, potentially affecting social interactions with peers in traditional schools.

Implementing a Flexible Approach

Hybrid Model: You can combine aspects of both traditional and year round schooling. For instance, you might have a shorter summer break but include additional breaks throughout the year.

Adjust Based on Needs: Choose the model that best fits your family's lifestyle and educational goals. Consider your child's learning style, your family's schedule, and any extracurricular activities when making this decision.

Starting the school year effectively involves thorough preparation, setting clear goals, and creating a supportive learning environment. Determining a schedule and pacing lessons requires understanding state laws, creating a balanced plan, and remaining flexible to adapt as needed. Whether you choose a traditional school year or year round schooling, the key is to create a structured yet adaptable approach that meets your child's needs and keeps them engaged in learning.

By carefully planning and maintaining flexibility, you can create a productive and enjoyable homeschooling experience that aligns with both educational requirements and your family's unique needs.

Managing Parental, Teaching, and Student Burnout

Parental Burnout

Definition: Parental burnout occurs when parents feel overwhelmed, exhausted, and emotionally drained from their caregiving and educational responsibilities. It can be caused by excessive demands, lack of support, and the pressure to meet various roles and expectations.

Signs: Chronic fatigue, irritability, feelings of inadequacy, and withdrawal from activities and responsibilities.

Management Strategies:

Set Realistic Expectations: Understand that homeschooling is a significant commitment, but perfection is not required. Set achievable goals and recognize your limits.

SelfCare: Prioritize self care by setting aside time for relaxation, hobbies, and social activities. Taking care of your wellbeing helps you be more effective as an educator and caregiver.

Seek Support: Join homeschooling support groups or forums to share experiences and gain advice. Consider professional help if needed.

Teaching Burnout

Definition: Teaching burnout is a state of physical, emotional, and mental exhaustion caused by the demands of teaching. It may involve feelings of frustration, decreased motivation, and a lack of enthusiasm for the subject matter.

Signs: Exhaustion, lack of motivation, reduced effectiveness, and increased stress.

Management Strategies:

Incorporate Breaks: Design a schedule that includes regular breaks throughout the day and week. This helps prevent fatigue and maintain enthusiasm.

Variety in Teaching Methods: Use a variety of teaching methods and materials to keep lessons engaging. Incorporate multimedia, handson activities, and different learning styles.

Professional Development: Engage in ongoing professional development to enhance teaching skills and gain new strategies. Utilize free resources and training programs available through your community or online.

Student Burnout

Definition: Student burnout occurs when students feel overwhelmed or disengaged from their learning due to excessive demands, lack of motivation, or stress.

Signs: Withdrawal from learning activities, lack of interest, fatigue, and frustration.

Management Strategies:

Balanced Schedule: Create a balanced schedule that includes time for breaks, extracurricular activities, and leisure. Avoid overwhelming students with too many demands.

Engaging Learning: Make learning enjoyable by incorporating interests and passions into the curriculum. Use project based learning and handson activities to keep students engaged.

Open Communication: Maintain open communication with your child about their feelings and challenges. Provide support and adjustments as needed.

Incorporating Breaks and Holidays

Setting a Schedule with Breaks

Daily Breaks: Include short breaks during the day to allow students and parents to recharge. For example, a 510 minute break after every 4560 minutes of focused work.

Weekly Breaks: Designate one or two days a week with reduced or no academic work to provide rest and relaxation.

Monthly Breaks: Plan for longer breaks each month to prevent burnout and provide opportunities for family activities and relaxation.

Incorporating Holidays into the Curriculum

Cultural and Religious Holidays: Recognize and incorporate cultural and religious holidays into the curriculum based on your family's traditions and beliefs. This can include special projects, readings, and activities related to the holiday.

Examples:

Christmas: Study the history and traditions of Christmas, including arts and crafts related to the holiday.

Hanukkah: Explore the significance of Hanukkah through storytelling, cooking traditional foods, and studying Jewish history.

Diwali: Learn about the cultural practices and stories associated with Diwali, and engage in related crafts and cooking.

BudgetFriendly Activities: Plan activities that align with your budget. Utilize free or low cost resources such as library books, community events, and online materials.

Examples:

Local Community Events: Participate in free or low cost holiday events hosted by local community centers, libraries, or cultural organizations.

DIY Projects: Create holiday themed projects at home using materials you already have.

Family Holiday Choices

Cultural and Personal Preferences: Choose holidays and traditions that resonate with your family's cultural background, budget, and personal preferences. This ensures that holiday activities are meaningful and engaging.

Integration with Curriculum: Integrate holiday themes into various subjects to enhance learning and make it relevant. For example, during a holiday season, incorporate related stories into reading lessons or explore historical aspects during history lessons.

Effectively managing parental, teaching, and student burnout involves creating a balanced schedule that includes regular breaks and holidays, incorporating family traditions, and maintaining open communication. By setting realistic expectations, engaging in self care, and being flexible with scheduling, you can create a supportive and effective homeschooling environment that fosters wellbeing and prevents burnout. Incorporating cultural and religious holidays into the curriculum not only enriches the learning experience but also respects and celebrates family traditions.

Using Family Culture, Religion, Heritage, and History in Education

Connecting Abstract Concepts to Concrete Examples

Personal Relevance: By tying educational concepts to a family's personal culture, religion, or heritage, students can relate abstract ideas to their own experiences. This relevance helps deepen understanding and retention.

Example: When studying ancient civilizations, a family with roots in a specific culture can explore the historical contributions of that culture, such as the art and architecture of Ancient Egypt if the family has Egyptian heritage. This connection makes the study of history more engaging and relevant.

Cultural Practices and Traditions: Incorporate cultural practices and traditions into lessons to provide concrete examples of abstract concepts.

Example: During a unit on agriculture, a family with farming traditions can demonstrate traditional farming techniques, discuss the significance of seasonal crops, and compare them to modern practices.

Utilizing Religion and Heritage

Religious and Historical Context: Understanding religious and historical contexts can provide valuable insights into broader educational themes, such as ethics, philosophy, or social structures.

Example: While studying world religions, a family can share their own religious practices and beliefs, discussing how these practices align with or differ from those of other religions. This creates a more nuanced understanding of the subject matter.

Family History: Explore family history to connect personal experiences with historical events or social changes.

Example: If a family has historical ties to a particular event, such as immigration or a significant historical movement, students can learn about the event through personal stories and primary sources, making the history more vivid and relatable.

The Role of Field Trips and Family Vacations

Enhancing Learning Through Field Trips

HandsOn Learning: Field trips provide practical experiences that reinforce classroom learning. They offer opportunities to see concepts in action, engage with experts, and explore relevant sites.

Example: Visiting a local historical site related to a lesson on colonial America allows students to see artifacts and learn about life during that time firsthand. If the family is visiting a region with cultural significance, they can participate in local festivals or traditions that align with their heritage.

RealWorld Connections: Field trips can help students connect their studies to real world contexts, enhancing understanding and interest.

Example: A trip to a museum with exhibits on ancient civilizations can complement a history lesson, while a visit to a botanical garden can reinforce concepts learned in a science unit on plant biology.

Integrating Family Vacations into Learning

Educational Exploration: Family vacations can be planned to align with educational goals, providing immersive learning experiences in different environments.

Example: A trip to a culturally significant region can offer students insights into the history, geography, and traditions of that area. This handson experience helps solidify their understanding of the concepts studied in class.

Cultural Exchange: Traveling exposes students to new cultures and perspectives, broadening their understanding of global diversity and fostering empathy.

Example: While traveling abroad, students can visit historical landmarks, participate in local customs, and learn about different cultural practices, enhancing their global awareness and appreciation for diversity.

Practical Tips for Incorporating Culture, Religion, and Heritage

Involve Family Members: Encourage family members to share their knowledge and experiences related to the educational topics being studied. This can include storytelling, cooking traditional dishes, or discussing family traditions.

Create Projects: Develop projects that integrate family culture or history with academic subjects. For example, students can create a family history timeline, a cultural recipe book, or a presentation on their family's historical contributions.

Document Learning: Keep a learning journal or portfolio that includes reflections on how personal culture, heritage, or family history has been incorporated into education. This helps students connect their learning to their identity and personal experiences.

Integrating a family's personal culture, religion, heritage, or history into education not only makes abstract concepts more concrete but also enriches the learning experience. By connecting educational material to personal and real world examples, and using field trips and family vacations as learning opportunities, students can gain a deeper, more meaningful understanding of the world. This approach fosters a strong connection between academic content and personal experience, enhancing engagement and retention while celebrating the unique aspects of each family's background.

Legal Considerations

Specific State Requirements

Notification: Most states require parents to notify the local education authority of their intent to homeschool. This may involve submitting an intent to homeschool form or letter, and some states may require an educational plan or proof of teaching qualifications.

Assessment: States differ in their requirements for assessing student progress. This could involve standardized tests, annual evaluations by a certified teacher, or periodic progress reports.

RecordKeeping: Parents are often required to keep detailed records of their child's education, including attendance logs, curriculum used, and samples of student work. This documentation ensures compliance with state regulations and can be useful for future educational transitions.

Homeschooling Associations

Local Associations: Many areas have local homeschooling associations that offer support, resources, and networking opportunities. These organizations can provide advice on legal requirements, curriculum choices, and local events.

National Organizations: National groups like the Home School Legal Defense Association (HSLDA) or the National Home Education Research Institute (NHERI) offer legal support, research, and advocacy for homeschooling families.

Diverse Learning Needs

Support for Learning Disabilities

Customized Instruction: Implement individualized education plans (IEPs) or 504 plans tailored to the child's specific learning needs. This may include specialized teaching methods, tools, and accommodations.

Professional Support: Seek evaluations and support from educational psychologists, special education specialists, or therapists to address specific learning disabilities.

Advanced Learners

Enrichment Activities: Provide challenging activities and advanced coursework to keep gifted students engaged. This could include accelerated learning programs, advanced books, or college level courses.

Independent Projects: Encourage self directed projects and research that align with the student's interests and talents.

Technology Integration

Educational Technology Tools

Apps and Software: Utilize educational apps and software that support various subjects and learning styles. Examples include language learning apps, math practice tools, and virtual science labs.

Online Courses: Incorporate online courses and resources from reputable providers to supplement traditional learning.

Balancing Screen Time

Scheduled Use: Set specific times for technology use to ensure it complements rather than dominates the learning experience.

HandsOn Activities: Balance digital learning with hands on activities like experiments, crafts, and physical exercises to promote a well rounded education.

Socialization Strategies

Social Opportunities

Homeschool Coops: Join or form local homeschool coops where families collaborate to provide group learning experiences and social opportunities for their children.

Extracurricular Activities: Enroll children in sports teams, clubs, or arts programs to ensure they interact with peers outside of the homeschool setting.

Networking with Other Homeschool Families

Community Events: Participate in local homeschool meetups, field trips, and educational fairs to build connections with other homeschooling families.

Online Communities: Engage with online forums and social media groups dedicated to homeschooling for support and resource sharing.

Curriculum Development

Customizing Curriculum

Student Interests: Tailor the curriculum to include topics that interest the student to enhance engagement and motivation. For example, if a child is passionate about space, incorporate astronomy into science lessons.

Flexibility: Adapt the curriculum as needed based on the student's progress and evolving interests.

Curriculum Evaluation

Regular Review: Periodically assess the effectiveness of the curriculum through student feedback, progress assessments, and personal observations.

Updates: Make necessary adjustments to the curriculum to address gaps, update resources, or introduce new subjects based on the student's needs.

Financial Planning

Funding Resources

Grants and Scholarships: Research and apply for grants or scholarships specifically available for homeschooling families. Some organizations offer financial aid for educational materials or extracurricular activities.

Tax Benefits: Explore potential tax benefits or deductions available for homeschooling expenses, such as curriculum costs and educational supplies.

CostSaving Tips

DIY Resources: Create your own educational materials, such as worksheets and visual aids, to save money on pre purchased resources.

Library Resources: Utilize local libraries for books, educational videos, and other resources that can supplement learning at minimal or no cost.

Health and Wellness

Mental Health

Open Communication: Foster an environment where children feel comfortable discussing their emotions and challenges. Address any signs of stress or anxiety promptly.

Support Services: Seek professional help if needed, including counseling or therapy, to support mental health and wellbeing.

Physical Activity

Incorporate Exercise: Include regular physical activities in the daily routine, such as outdoor play, sports, or exercise routines.

Health Education: Teach students about healthy living, nutrition, and exercise as part of their overall education.

Future Planning

Transitioning to Higher Education

College Applications: Guide students through the college application process, including preparing for standardized tests, writing personal statements, and meeting application deadlines.

Dual Enrollment: Explore dual enrollment options for high school students to earn college credits while still in homeschool.

Career Readiness

Career Exploration: Provide opportunities for career exploration through internships, job shadowing, or vocational training.

Skill Development: Focus on developing essential skills such as communication, problem solving, and time management.

Community and Cultural Integration

Cultural Sensitivity

Global Awareness: Incorporate lessons on world cultures, religions, and customs to promote global understanding and sensitivity.

Inclusive Curriculum: Ensure that the curriculum reflects diverse perspectives and experiences.

Community Engagement

Service Projects: Engage students in community service projects to foster a sense of civic responsibility and empathy.

Local Partnerships: Collaborate with local organizations and businesses to provide students with real world learning experiences.

Parent Support

SelfCare for Parents

Stress Management: Practice stress management techniques such as mindfulness, exercise, and regular breaks to maintain wellbeing.

Support Networks: Connect with other homeschooling parents for mutual support and shared experiences.

Professional Development

Workshops and Courses: Attend workshops, webinars, and online courses to enhance teaching skills and stay updated on educational best practices.

Local Resources: Explore local educational institutions or community centers that offer professional development opportunities for parents.

Choosing to embark on a K12 humane homeschool journey is a profound decision that reflects a commitment to your child's holistic development and wellbeing. It is a path that offers unparalleled flexibility, allowing you to tailor education to fit your child's unique needs, interests, and strengths. By creating a learning environment that honors diversity, fosters critical thinking, and integrates personal culture and values, you are not just providing an education but nurturing a lifelong love of learning.

In a humane homeschool, you become more than just an educator; you are a partner in your child's intellectual and emotional growth, integrating lessons with real world experiences and personal significance. This approach honors their individual learning style, encourages self efficacy, and builds a strong, supportive relationship between you and your child.

However, if your family decides that homeschooling is no longer the right fit, it is essential to remember that your choice, whatever it may be, is valid and best for your family at that time. Education is not a one size fits all endeavor; it evolves with the needs of the student and the family. Transitioning to a new educational setting, whether public, private, or an alternative, is also a responsible and informed decision that reflects your commitment to finding the best path for your child's continued growth.

Ultimately, the best school choice is one that aligns with your family's values, needs, and circumstances. Whether you continue with a humane homeschool or explore other educational options, your decision is an affirmation of your dedication to providing the best possible learning environment for your child. Embrace the journey with confidence, knowing that your choices are made with care, consideration, and the best interests of your child at heart.

Resources:

Curriculum and Lesson Planning

"Cox Campus." Cox Campus, https://www.coxcampus.org/.

"Khan Academy." Khan Academy, https://www.khanacademy.org/.

"Education.com." Education.com, https://www.education.com/.

"Twinkl." Twinkl, https://www.twinkl.com/.

"PBS LearningMedia." PBS LearningMedia, https://www.pbslearningmedia.org/.

Neurodiversity and Inclusive Education

"Understood.org." Understood, https://www.understood.org/.

"The Center for Neurodiversity." The Center for Neurodiversity, https://neurodiversitycenter.org/.

"The National Center for Learning Disabilities (NCLD)." NCLD, https://www.ncld.org/.

"Neurodiversity Celebration Week." Neurodiversity Celebration Week, https://www.neurodiversitycelebrationweek.com/.

Environmental Education and Sustainability

"Project Learning Tree." Project Learning Tree, https://www.plt.org/.

"Nature Lab." The Nature Conservancy, https://www.nature.org/enus/getinvolved/howtohelp/naturelab/.

"National Geographic Kids." National Geographic Kids, https://kids.nationalgeographic.com/.

Professional Development

"Microsoft Learn." Microsoft Learn, https://learn.microsoft.com/enus/training/.

"YouTube Educational Channels." YouTube, https://www.youtube.com/.

Social and Emotional Learning

"Second Step." Second Step, https://www.secondstep.org/.

"MindUp." MindUp, https://mindup.org/.

Field Trips and Extracurricular Activities

"Museum Finder." Museum Finder, https://www.museumfinder.com/.

"North American Association for Environmental Education." NAAEE, https://www.naaee.org/.

Health and Wellness

"American Academy of Pediatrics." American Academy of Pediatrics, https://pediatrics.aappublications.org/.

"HealthyChildren.org." HealthyChildren, https://www.healthychildren.org/.

Community and Support Networks

"Homeschool Legal Defense Association (HSLDA)." HSLDA, https://hslda.org/.

"The WellTrained Mind Community." The WellTrained Mind Community, https://forums.welltrainedmind.com/.

"School Choice Week." School Choice Week, https://schoolchoiceweek.com/.

Multisensory and HandsOn Learning

"The Imagination Tree." The Imagination Tree, https://theimaginationtree.com/.

"TinkerLab." TinkerLab, https://tinkerlab.com/.

Educational Technology

"Edutopia." Edutopia, https://www.edutopia.org/.

"Common Sense Education." Common Sense Education, https://www.commonsense.org/education/.

Also by Astronomical Tutor

Astronomical Learning
Humane Homeschooling

Watch for more at https://sites.google.com/view/astronomicaltutor/home.

About the Author

Mrs. Deanna, known as Astronomical Tutor on Instagram, is a passionate advocate for inclusive education and empowerment through knowledge. Her journey as a parent, homeschool educator, virtual tutor, and now an author has been driven by a commitment to unlocking the full potential of every individual.

With her self-published book, Astronomical Learning, on family and community engagement, structured literacy, math instruction, with a strength-based approach, Mrs. Deanna offers a transformative perspective on education.

Embracing neurodiversity as a biological reality, she challenges the limitations of traditional education systems, advocating for tailored approaches that honor the unique strengths and abilities of each learner.

Through her work, Mrs. Deanna strives to create a world where education is not a one-size-fits-all model but a dynamic process that celebrates diversity and fosters growth. Follow her on Instagram as Astronomical Tutor to join the journey towards a more inclusive and empowering educational landscape.

Read more at https://sites.google.com/view/astronomicaltutor/home.